mother & daughter
# closer
to God and to each other

## Susie Shellenberger

Tyndale House Publishers, Inc., Carol Stream, Illinois

*Closer*

ISBN: 1-58997-356-9

A Focus on the Family book published by
Tyndale House Publishers, Carol Stream, Illinois 60188

TYNDALE is a registered trademark of Tyndale House Publishers, Inc. Tyndale's quill logo is a trademark of Tyndale House Publishers, Inc.

All Scripture quotations, unless otherwise indicated, are taken from the *Holy Bible, New International Version*®. NIV®. Copyright © 1973, 1978, 1984 by International Bible Society. Used by permission of Zondervan Publishing House. All rights reserved. Scripture quotations marked (NASB) are taken from the *New American Standard Bible*®. Copyright The Lockman Foundation 1960, 1962, 1963, 1968, 1971, 1972, 1973, 1975, 1977, 1995. Used by permission. (www.Lockman.org). Scripture quotations marked (TLB) are taken from *The Living Bible* (paraphrase) Copyright © 1971. Used by permission of Tyndale House Publishers, Carol Stream, Illinois 60188. All rights reserved.

Editor: Lissa Halls Johnson
Cover designed by: Jennifer Lund
Cover photo: © by Stockbyte/Getty Images. All rights reserved.
Interior designed by: Jeff Lane, Smith/Lane Associates
Interior photos: Sarah Bolser: Flipflop and beach tote icons, 10, 17, 22, 25, 29, 33, 34, 37, 41, 43, 45, 52, 53, 55, 56, 58, 61, 66, 68, 69, 72, 75, 79, 83, 91, 93, 95, 97, 101, 105, 108, 111, 112, 125, 128, 130, 138, 144, 151, 154, 157, 160, 161, 165, 169, 172
Jeff Lane: 14, 31, 82
Melinda Lane: 110, 113

Printed in the United States of America
1  2  3  4  5  6  7  8  9  /11 10  09  08  07  06

The author is represented by the literary agency of WordServe Literary Group, Ltd., 10152 S. Knoll Circle, Highlands Ranch, CO  80130.

Library of Congress Cataloging-in-Publication Data

Shellenberger, Susie.
    Closer : to God and to each other / Susie Shellenberger.
        p. cm.
    "A Focus on the Family book"--T.p. verso.
    ISBN 1-58997-356-9
    1. Mothers and daughters--Religious aspects--Christianity. 2. Female friendship--Religious aspects--Christianity. 3. Christian women--Religious life.   I. Title.
BV4529.18.S53 2005
248.8'43--dc22

2005018072

*Dedicated to:*

My mother, Marjorie Shellenberger

(April 17, 1923 – August 3, 2003)

She gave me love, confidence, and passion for God.

Susie Shellenberger with her mom, Marjorie, in 1997.

My second mother, Lawana Isaacs Shellenberger

(October 15, 1925 –)

She gives me love, demonstrates godliness, and completes our family.

Lawana Isaacs Shellenberger with her daughters Shelley Nichols and Jamie Horowitz.

# Closer

By Susie Shellenberger

## Read This First!

### Start right here.

### Begin at this point.

### Don't read anything else until you've read this.

### Don't turn the page yet.

### This is where you want to be.

### Original starting point.

*Welcome!*

Come on in a little closer.

Yeah, you.

I want to talk to the two of you.

*I'm so thrilled about the journey you've decided to take together through this book. Why? Because there's something powerful that happens when moms and daughters connect on a deep level, where hearts are safely shared, and as a result, become knit together in love and intimacy. By the end of this book, you'll find out how exciting it is to be closer to each other and closer to Christ.*

*Girls, maybe you don't know it, but one of the most important relationships you'll ever have (besides with God and your future husband) is with your mom. And moms, you already know how important it is to have a special relationship with your daughters. Together you're going to discover what an extraordinary thing it is to be a mom and daughter who are truly bonded together in Christ.*

*You'll notice there aren't any chapters in this book. Only gab fests. Who needs chapters when you're going to talk your way through the pages? So instead of being confined by chapters, you'll find fun, freeing, thought-provoking gab fests. This is your chance to talk and talk and talk and talk. With each other.*

*So . . . your goals for this book:*

*1. Grow closer to Christ.*

*2. Grow closer to each other.*

*3. Grow closer to Christ together.*

*If you've met those goals after reading this book, you'll find there's no limit to what can happen in your lives! God can do mighty things through a committed mom and an on-fire daughter. He can spark laughter in the midst of tears. Rays of sun through a downpour. Obedience in spite of miscommunication. Genuine love right in the middle of a disagreement. Unity through prayer. Power through unity.*

*Let God forever impact you by blessing your special mom/daughter relationship. Go ahead and thank Him ahead of time – before you even open the book – for what He's going to do!*

*Your Friend,*

Susie Shellenberger

# Here we go!

Every time you see a beach tote, that's where Mom  answers the question. And every time you see a pair of flip-flops, that's where the daughter gets to share. But even that isn't a hard-and-fast rule. Mix it up! Answer each other's questions! Guess how you think the other will answer. Have fun with them. Take as long as you want to answer them. All I want to suggest is this: Be real. Be authentic. Tell the truth about yourself. About what you think and feel. It might be scary. But try it for me, okay?

Before we start our first Gab Fest, do this exercise. It might help you as you go through the rest of the book!

Moms and daughters often see things differently. They can look at the same situation and both have a completely different take on it. Dig into the following scenario and discuss the difference between a mom's viewpoint and a daughter's take.

Jamie's term paper is due on December 15. She's known about it since the first of September. It's now November 15, and she still hasn't started it.

"Mom," Jamie says, nearly dancing in place, her eyes shining, "Ashley invited me to go skiing with her family this weekend. We're going to stay in their cabin. We'll ski Saturday and Sunday, and I'll be back Sunday evening. Can I go?" She wants to say more, but bites her lip.

"I think you'd better say no and get started on your term paper, Jamie. It's due in just a few weeks. You haven't even begun your research."

"Mom. You're stressing for nothing. It's no big deal. I have plenty of time." Jamie smiles, trying not to beg or sound pushy. "I already have my topic, and the paper has to be only six pages. I can go skiing this weekend and work on the paper next weekend."

*What's the danger of your daughter waiting another week to start her term paper?*

......................................................................

......................................................................

Why is Mom getting stressed? You still have a month to get it done.

— — — — — — — — — — — — — — — — — — —

— — — — — — — — — — — — — — — — — — —

— — — — — — — — — — — — — — — — — — —

Jamie had a great time skiing, but came home sick and missed two days of school. She spent the following weekend catching up on homework and studying for makeup tests. The church retreat is right around the corner, and Jamie's on the leadership council.

Mom sits on the edge of Jamie's bed while Jamie lies there, working on her homework. "Jamie, I'm thinking it isn't a good idea for you to go on the retreat next weekend."

"You're kidding, right?" Jamie says, totally shocked. "I've helped put it together. Mom, we've been planning it all semester. I've got to be there."

"What about your term paper?"

"Not a problem. We get back from the retreat at noon on Sunday. I'll start as soon as I get back."

 Though you have every intention of starting the paper on Sunday afternoon, what are some things that could interfere with your plan?

_____

_____

_____

_____

*You've seen Jamie work under pressure. You know she can do it, but it makes you nervous. You like to have things planned and completed in advance. Should you give her the benefit of the doubt again and allow her to partici-pate in the retreat?*

*What are the reasons behind your answer? (Be as detailed as you can.)*

........................................................

........................................................

........................................................

........................................................

Really listen to what your mom is saying. Can you see and understand your mom's point of view without being defensive? Can you respect her view even though it's different from your own?

_____

_____

*Do you appreciate the differences between you and your daughter? Can you teach her how to set goals and follow through on them without appearing to be mistrusting or nagging?*

..................................................................

..................................................................

..................................................................

..................................................................

 Perhaps you're a whiz writer and research expert and really can pull off a term paper with lightning speed. God desires that you honor and respect your parental authority. Even though you may be able to pull this project off with a limited amount of time, will you respect and honor your mom and get started on it much earlier than you really need to?

You can prove your ability to work quickly by starting your next project way early and completing it in advance of the deadline. This will show your mom that you really can produce under pressure.

*Your daughter may have grandiose dreams of being able to complete a huge project in a limited amount of time, but perhaps you've seen her attempt this in the past, and she's been disappointed with the results. Remind her that you believe in her, and you'll do everything you can to help her work well under pressure. But also help her realize the danger of waiting too long because of unforeseen circumstances: illness, unexpected home-*

*work, other want-to-do invitations (dinner, a sleepover, a movie, shopping with friends), car problems, etc.*

So what did you learn about each other? Do you think exactly alike? Do you see the situation the same? In the next few pages, you'll not only learn how each other thinks; you'll also learn how to respect and appreciate the differences you have.

......................................................................................

......................................................................................

......................................................................................

......................................................................................

......................................................................................

Take a moment—right now—before you actually dive inside these pages, to ask God to bless your journey together through this book. And go ahead: Thank Him ahead of time for how He's going to draw you closer to each other and closer to Him.

# Table of Contents

Take turns reading the following scripture. Each time there's a paragraph break, change readers.

*Now there was a man of the Pharisees named Nicodemus, a member of the Jewish ruling council. He came to Jesus at night and said, "Rabbi, we know you are a teacher who has come from God. For no one could perform the miraculous signs you are doing if God were not with him."*

*In reply Jesus declared, "I tell you the truth, no one can see the kingdom of God unless he is born again."*

*"How can a man be born when he is old?" Nicodemus asked. "Surely he cannot enter*

GAB FEST #1:

# Basic Christianity

*a second time into his mother's womb to be born!"*

*Jesus answered, "I tell you the truth, no one can enter the kingdom of God unless he is born of water and the Spirit. Flesh gives birth to flesh, but the Spirit gives birth to spirit. You should not be surprised at my saying, 'You must be born again.' "* (John 3:1-7)

Before we introduce ourselves to Nicodemus, let's first take a peek at the Pharisees—the group to which he belonged. During the time Jesus walked on earth, the Pharisees were a powerful branch of the Jewish religious community.

List a few special groups to which you've belonged in the past.

4-H

4-H
awanas
baseball
band

The Pharisees were extremely strict about obeying God's laws, and the traditions they had established to go along with God's laws to help themselves and others to get it right. While that may sound helpful, Jesus actually said some pretty harsh things to them. Grab your Bible and flip to Matthew, chapter 23. Each of you list two things for which Christ condemned the Pharisees.

1. _ _ _ _ _ _ _ _ _ _ _ _ _ _ _ _ _ _ _ _ _ _ _ _ _ _

2. _ _ _ _ _ _ _ _ _ _ _ _ _ _ _ _ _ _ _ _ _ _ _ _ _ _

1 . . . . . . . . . . . . . . . . . . . . . . . . . . . . . . . . . . . . . . . . . . . . . . . . . . . . .

2 . . . . . . . . . . . . . . . . . . . . . . . . . . . . . . . . . . . . . . . . . . . . . . . . . . . . .

The Pharisees thought of themselves as the religious experts of their time. How do you feel when someone around you tries to convince you that he/she is an expert at something—and probably isn't?

. . . . . . . . . . . . . . . . . . . . . . . . . . . . . . . . . . . . . . . . . . . . . . . . . . . . . . . . . . . .

. . . . . . . . . . . . . . . . . . . . . . . . . . . . . . . . . . . . . . . . . . . . . . . . . . . . . . . . . . . .

. . . . . . . . . . . . . . . . . . . . . . . . . . . . . . . . . . . . . . . . . . . . . . . . . . . . . . . . . . . .

. . . . . . . . . . . . . . . . . . . . . . . . . . . . . . . . . . . . . . . . . . . . . . . . . . . . . . . . . . . .

. . . . . . . . . . . . . . . . . . . . . . . . . . . . . . . . . . . . . . . . . . . . . . . . . . . . . . . . . . . .

. . . . . . . . . . . . . . . . . . . . . . . . . . . . . . . . . . . . . . . . . . . . . . . . . . . . . . . . . . . .

How can you tell if one is truly an expert at what he claims to know?

. . . . . . . . . . . . . . . . . . . . . . . . . . . . . . . . . . . . . . . . . . . . . . . . . . . . . . . . . . . .

. . . . . . . . . . . . . . . . . . . . . . . . . . . . . . . . . . . . . . . . . . . . . . . . . . . . . . . . . . . .

. . . . . . . . . . . . . . . . . . . . . . . . . . . . . . . . . . . . . . . . . . . . . . . . . . . . . . . . . . . .

Do you consider Jesus Christ to be an expert?

If so, at what?

Okay. Let's check out Nicodemus. He approached Jesus. That's good! Jesus wants us to approach Him with everything that concerns us. What have you approached Christ with during the last week?

Nicodemus approached Jesus, but he approached Him at night so we now know him as "Nick at Nite." Why do you suppose Nick chose this particular time to drum up a conversation with Jesus? (Mark all that apply.)

❑ He was allergic to sunlight.

❑ He was frightened.

❑ He was embarrassed.

❑ He wasn't wearing the right clothes.

❏ He didn't want to risk his reputation.

❏ He had a day job and couldn't get off work.

❏ He had trouble getting his chariot to start.

❏ Other _ _ _ _ _ _ _ _ _ _ _

_ _ _ _ _ _ _ _ _ _ _ _ _ _

_ _ _ _ _ _ _ _ _ _ _ _ _ _

_ _ _ _ _ _ _ _ _ _ _ _ _ _ _ _ _ _ _ _ _ _

_ _ _ _ _ _ _ _ _ _ _ _ _ _ _ _ _ _ _ _ _ _

Why did Nicodemus want to talk to Jesus?

................................................................

................................................................

................................................................

................................................................

Take a moment and pretend you're Nicodemus. Introduce yourself to your mom.

_ _ _ _ _ _ _ _ _ _ _ _ _ _ _ _ _ _ _ _ _ _ _ _ _

_ _ _ _ _ _ _ _ _ _ _ _ _ _ _ _ _ _ _ _ _ _ _ _ _

_ _ _ _ _ _ _ _ _ _ _ _ _ _ _ _ _ _ _ _ _ _ _ _ _

_ _ _ _ _ _ _ _ _ _ _ _ _ _ _ _ _ _ _ _ _ _ _ _ _

*closer*

*Mom, how would you share with Nicodemus about becoming a Christian?*

..................................................
..................................................
..................................................
..................................................
..................................................

As Jesus answered Nicodemus, how many times did He emphasize that He was telling the truth? ☐

Why is that important?

..................................................
..................................................
..................................................

Grab your Bible and check out John 14:6. What three things does Jesus claim to be?

1. .................................
2. .................................
3. .................................

How many different paths does Jesus say lead to the Father? ☐

*How many differ-
ent paths did
Jesus tell Nicodemus he
could take in becoming
a Christian?* ☐

If you both inked a
bold number ONE in
your box, you're cor-
rect. There's really
only ONE WAY to live
forever—and that's
through forgiveness of sins from Jesus Christ.
He calls this being BORN AGAIN.

*Mom, what are two significant memories you have of your
daughter's birth?*

..........................................................................................

..........................................................................................

What's the earliest birthday you remember?

..........................................................................................

What's the earliest birthday gift you remember receiving?

..........................................................................................

Being BORN AGAIN is something that's impossible
by human standards. (Is Mom groaning at the thought?) But

Jesus doesn't think the way we think. He was thinking in spiritual terms. He was talking about the Holy Spirit breathing life into our unborn spirit. When we allow Him to do that in us, our spirit is awakened and we are reborn into an awareness of spiritual things, and a connection with God. We become a new person if we've taken Christ's death on the cross as payment to forgive our sins.

In Jesus' conversation with Nicodemus, He answered,

*"I tell you the truth, no one can enter the kingdom of God unless he is born of water and the Spirit."*

The water Jesus referred to could mean being baptized, and it could also refer to a mother's water breaking before her baby is born. Being born in the Spirit means becoming aware and obedient to the Holy Spirit working in our lives.

*Mom, how long after your water broke was your daughter born?*

...................................................................

 Have you ever thanked your mom for giving you life? Take a moment to do that right now.

closer

## Take a Break!

You deserve it. Look how much you've just completed. Whew! Have fun together. Go shopping, swimming, biking, napping, cooking, whatever! Then enjoy the next page.

## ❀ Did You Know? ❀

❀ Women in the Trobriand Islands don't need to bother with curling their eyelashes. Here's why: On this particular island, when a man falls in love with a woman, he customarily bites off her eyelashes.

❀ Women in nudist camps tend to use more makeup than women elsewhere.

❀ Cleopatra daubed perfume between each of her toes. When she set out to meet Mark Antony, history tells us that she even sprinkled perfume all over the sails of her barge.

❀ One hundred years ago, a woman thought herself to be particularly gifted if she were one who grew a faint moustache. That light down on the female face was considered extremely attractive.

❀ Women of the Tiwi tribe in the South Pacific are married at birth.

❀ One of Queen Victoria's wedding gifts was a piece of cheese three meters in diameter and weighing in at 1,000 pounds.

❀ It was considered unfashionable for Venetian women, during the Renaissance, to have anything but silvery-blonde hair.

❀ The two highest IQs ever recorded (on a standard test) both belong to women.

## Journal

*Mom, you go first. Take this entire first page and explain how much you love your daughter and how incredibly special and unique she is. Feel free to attach a photo of the two of you together, draw stick figures representing the two of you, or place stickers or something fun on this page. Be creative!*

..................................................................................
..................................................................................
..................................................................................
..................................................................................
..................................................................................
..................................................................................
..................................................................................
..................................................................................
..................................................................................
..................................................................................
..................................................................................
..............................
..............................
..............................
..............................
..............................
..............................

Okay, your turn. Use this page to tell your mom how much you love her. Point out the special things you see in her life and let her know specifics for which you're grateful. Be as creative as you can. Tape or glue photos, cut words out of magazines to make your message, whatever!

closer

# Back on Course

As you read about Nicodemus and his search to become a Christian, was there something you couldn't help but think?

_____ a. Yeah, I know a lot about God, but I don't really know Him personally.

_____ b. I'm sure glad I have a growing relationship with God.

_____ c. I'm not sure where I stand with God, but I'd sure like to find out.

_____ d. I've already committed my life to God, but I've taken some backward steps, and I need to recommit some things to Him.

If you've never placed your faith in Christ, asked Him to forgive your sins, or developed an actual relationship with Him, you can do that right here, right now!

You can either say this prayer together or you can repeat it one at a time. If you're confident that you already have an active, growing relationship with Christ, skip this part and jump down to the beach towel.

*Dear Jesus,*

*I believe You're the Son of God and that You left the glory of heaven to invade my world with love, grace, and forgiveness. Someone has to pay for my sins. It's either me . . . or You. And You love me so incredibly much, You allowed Yourself to be tortured and crucified on a cross to pay for everything I've done wrong.*

*Thank You! Oh, dear Jesus, I don't deserve that kind of love. I know I could never be good enough to earn Your forgiveness, so I simply thank You for the wonderful gift of Your life for my sins.*

*Dear Jesus, will You forgive me for everything I've done wrong? I'm so sorry! I'm so sorry I've demanded my own way, my own rights, and have done things that have broken Your heart and hurt others.*

*Thank You for hearing my prayer of confession right now. I admit it: I'm a sinner. But Jesus, I accept Your forgiveness for my sins. I invite You to come into my heart and take control of my life. I'm choosing to live for You. I give You my life. Thank You, Jesus! Thank You for making me a brand-new person in You.*
*Amen.*

If you prayed this prayer, I want you to initial and date this page.

As a testimony of your new faith, you'll want to talk with your pastor about baptism. This is a wonderful way to show others what Christ has done for you.

Let's look at a snapshot of someone else who asked Jesus about eternal life. We don't know him by his name—only by his label: **The Rich Young Man**. His story is found in Matthew 19:16-24. Jesus told him that obeying the Ten Commandments was important in Christian living, but He also told him to do something else. What was it?

_____ a. Join a church.

_____ b. Work harder to earn more money and give extra to the poor.

_____ c. Sell his possessions and give the money to the poor.

_____ d. Serve at the local soup kitchen.

_____ e. Dress nicer.

Jesus wasn't saying it's a sin to be rich, but He was emphasizing that it takes more than following commandments to be a genuine follower of His. It takes **total surrender**. Jesus knew the man's bank account was the most important thing in his life. You see, Christ not only wants our obedience (following the Ten Commandments); He also wants a **relationship with us** that's based on **total surrender**.

I can be **assured** that I'm a Christian if:

_____ a. I know a lot about God and treat others kindly.

_____ b. I'm a good person.

_____ c. I've repented of my sins, asked Christ for forgiveness, turned my life over to Him, and am living in obedience to Him.

_____ d. I go to church regularly.

I hope you checked the third option, because that really is the key to **establishing** and **maintaining** a relationship with Jesus Christ. The rich young man refused to give Jesus control of his money, and therefore his heart and his life.

What area in your life is the most difficult to give Christ control of?

...........................

...........................

...........................

...........................

Why? What are you most afraid of?

...........................

...........................

...........................

closer

What difference would it make if you did commit everything to Christ?

...........................................................................

...........................................................................

...........................................................................

...........................................................................

What risks are there in doing that?

...........................................................................

...........................................................................

...........................................................................

...........................................................................

Describe someone you know who lives in total surrender
to Jesus Christ. How is his/her life different from
others?

...........................................................................

...........................................................................

...........................................................................

...........................................................................

...........................................................................

...........................................................................

...........................................................................

How do you know this person lives in total surrender to Christ? What clues does his/her lifestyle give that suggest such a commitment?

.......................................................................................

.......................................................................................

.......................................................................................

.......................................................................................

## Take a Break!

You deserve it. Look how much you've just completed. Whew! Have fun together. Make some pottery, go fishing, drink some lemonade, go walking, whatever!

# Did You Know?

🌸 Betsy Ross is the only real person to ever have been the head on a Pez dispenser.

🌸 The sound of E.T. walking was made by a woman squishing her hands in jelly.

🌸 Forty percent of women have hurled footwear at a man.

🌸 Eighty-five percent of women wear the wrong bra size.

🌸 Nearly one in three U.S. women colors her hair.

🌸 Nine percent of women and eight percent of men have had cosmetic surgery.

🌸 Fifty-three percent of women won't leave the house without makeup on.

🌸 Fifty-eight percent of women paint their nails regularly.

🌸 Fifty-six percent of women do the bills in a marriage.

🌸 Men can read smaller print than women, but women can hear better.

🌸 Eleanor Roosevelt was the only First Lady to carry a loaded revolver.

🌸 Women don't get hiccups as often as men.

🌸 The cruise liner *Queen Elizabeth 2* moves only 49.5 feet for each gallon of fuel that it burns.

# GAB FEST #2:

# Does God Really Have My Heart?

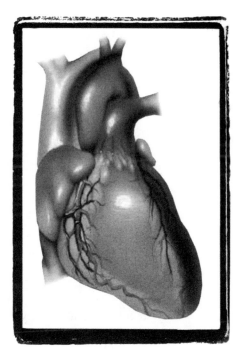

Ready for a little mom/daughter competition? Take one minute and see who can create the longest list of songs with the word *heart* in the titles.

. . . . . . . . . . . . . . . . . . . . . . . . . . . . . . . .        _ _ _ _ _ _ _ _ _ _ _ _

. . . . . . . . . . . . . . . . . . . . . . . . . . . . . . . .        _ _ _ _ _ _ _ _ _ _ _ _

. . . . . . . . . . . . . . . . . . . . . . . . . . . . . . . .        _ _ _ _ _ _ _ _ _ _ _ _

. . . . . . . . . . . . . . . . . . . . . . . . . . . . . . . .        _ _ _ _ _ _ _ _ _ _ _ _

. . . . . . . . . . . . . . . . . . . . . . . . . . . . . . . .        _ _ _ _ _ _ _ _ _ _ _ _

. . . . . . . . . . . . . . . . . . . . . . . . . . . . . . . .        _ _ _ _ _ _ _ _ _ _ _ _

................................    — — — — — — — — — —

................................    — — — — — — — — — —

................................    — — — — — — — — — —

................................    — — — — — — — — — —

No doubt about it, your heart is important! But how much do you really know about your heart?

_____ a. Uh, I know it beats inside my chest.

_____ b. It beats faster when Jason walks by.

_____ c. It skips a beat when my history teacher announces a surprise quiz.

_____ d. It hurts reallyreallyreally bad when it's broken.

_____ e. Other — — — — — — — — — — — — — — — — — — — — — —

— — — — — — — — — — — — — — — — — — — — — — — — — —

Your heart is not only **super important**; it's also quite busy!

Did you know your heart is responsible for pumping blood to every single cell in your entire body? That really is a big job!

_____ a. So that's why I'm so tired!

_____ b. Okay, so when I'm asked a question in class and I don't know the answer, I'm just going to say, "Sorry. Can't talk right now. My heart's busy."

_____ c. So now I have an excuse to sleep in, right?

_____ d. At least my heart has a job. Wish I could find one!

And since **your heart is busy** pumping blood to every cell in your body, you're probably thinking:

_____ a. Yikes! Sure hope it doesn't miss a cell.

_____ b. How many cells do I have?

_____ c. What if my heart forgets to do its job someday? (Cuz, you know . . . sometimes I forget to take out the trash, and I forget where I put my car keys, and we won't even talk about where I left my beach tote.)

There's no way I can tell you **exactly how many cells** are in your body, because your body is constantly changing. Cells die and others are formed. And the number of cells for each person **varies** according to her size. But we can give you **the scoop** on what scientists have said.

Some say **the human body** has 50 million million cells (that equals 50 trillion)! Others say you have 10 million. And Science NetLinks says you have 10 to the 14th power (or 100 trillion) cells. So though we don't know exactly how many cells you have, we do know you have a lot! **A whole gob**. A big bunch.

It's surprising how small the heart really is—considering how much work it has to do. **An average adult's heart** is about the size of a **clenched fist** and weighs approximately 11 ounces.

### Here are a few more fun facts about your heart:

💜 The human heart pumps a million barrels of blood during an average lifetime.

💜 Your heart beats around 40,000,000 times a year.

💜 The blood of a human makes a complete circuit of the body every 23 seconds.

Now that you know what **scientists** have said about the **heart**, let's check out what the **Bible** has to say. (Take turns reading the following scriptures out loud.)

*Above all else, guard your **heart**, for it is the wellspring of life. (Proverbs 4:23)*

*Love the LORD your God with all your **heart** and with all your **soul** and with all your **strength**. (Deuteronomy 6:5)*

How can you actually do what the above verses tell you?

............................................................

............................................................

............................................................

Give a specific example of how someone you know loves God with all her heart, soul, and strength.

..........................................................................

..........................................................................

..........................................................................

..........................................................................

..........................................................................

*Mom, identify a time when your heart was broken. Share with your daughter how you worked through the heartache.*

..........................................................................

..........................................................................

..........................................................................

..........................................................................

..........................................................................

..........................................................................

..........................................................................

..........................................................................

Share a time when your heart was so full and happy you thought you'd burst.

— — — — — — — — — — — — — — — — — — — —

— — — — — — — — — — — — — — — — — — — —

closer

---------------------------------------------

---------------------------------------------

---------------------------------------------

---------------------------------------------

*Take a moment to pray out loud for your daughter. Thank God that she's your daughter, ask Him for wisdom in guiding her, and tell Him you want to bring out the very best in her.*

Take a moment to pray out loud for your mom. Thank God that she's your mom, ask Him for wisdom in communicating with her, and tell Him you want to bring out the very best in her.

## Take a Break!

You deserve it. Look how much you've just completed. Whew! Have fun together. Go swimming, make brownies for the neighbors, act out songs from a musical, whatever!

closer

# Some Important Women in History

**Cleopatra** (68 B.C. – 30 B.C.) became Queen of Egypt at age 18.

**Joan of Arc** (1412 – 1431) helped the French defeat the English and was burned at the stake.

**Queen Elizabeth I** (1533 – 1603) Queen of England. During her reign, there were great achievements in writing and peace in England.

**Pocahontas** (1595 – 1617) saved Captain John Smith's life.

**Abigail Adams** (1744 – 1818) Wife of President John Adams, mother of President John Quincy Adams. She was influential in the beginnings of the United States as a nation, and she supported women's rights.

**Betsy Ross** (1752 – 1836) American seamstress. According to legend, she made the first American flag.

**Mary Ludwig Hays McCauley** "Molly Pitcher" (1754 – 1832) brought water to the soldiers in the field. When her husband was injured on a Revolutionary War battlefield, Molly took over his gun.

**Deborah Sampson** (1760 – 1827) fought in the Revolutionary War, pretending to be a man.

**Sacagawea** (1787? – 1812) Guide and interpreter for the Lewis & Clark Expedition.

**Sojourner Truth** (1797 – 1883) African American who spoke out against slavery and for the rights of women.

**Harriet Beecher Stowe** (1811 – 1896) wrote *Uncle Tom's Cabin* about slavery in the South. More than 500,000 copies were sold in the United States, which helped to bring the nation's attention to the horrors of slavery.

**Lucy Stone** (1818 – 1893) One of the first women in the United States to earn a college degree, graduating first in her class from Oberlin College in 1847.

**Susan B. Anthony** (1820 – 1906) formed the National Woman's Suffrage

Association. She was the first woman to have her picture on an American coin (silver dollar).

**Marie Curie** (1867 – 1934) As a scientist, she won two Nobel prizes, one with her husband's work on radioactivity, and one on her own. She discovered radium and polonium.

## Back on Course

Grab a brownie and let's keep going!

*Trust in the LORD with all your heart and lean not on your own understanding; in all your ways acknowledge him, and he will make your paths straight. (Proverbs 3:5-6)*

*God has promised straight paths if we acknowledge Him with our entire lives. Identify a time in your life when you've experienced a crooked path and a time when you've experienced a straight path. (What was the specific situation? What made the difference between one path being crooked and the other being straight?)*

.................................

.................................

.................................

.................................

.................................

.................................

.................................

How can you "trust in the Lord with all your heart"?

..............................................................
..............................................................
..............................................................
..............................................................
..............................................................
..............................................................

*Mom, do you notice specific areas in your daughter's life in which she finds it difficult to trust God?*

..............................................................
..............................................................
..............................................................
..............................................................
..............................................................

What areas in your mom's life do you see that she clearly trusts God?

_____
_____
_____
_____
_____

*closer*

*Create in me a pure heart, O God, and renew a steadfast spirit within me. (Psalm 51:10)*

What's a steadfast spirit? Do you know someone with a steadfast spirit? Describe him/her.

.....................................

.....................................

.....................................

.....................................

.........................................................

.........................................................

.........................................................

.........................................................

*Mom, identify a situation in which you've seen a steadfast spirit in your daughter.*

.........................................................

.........................................................

.........................................................

.........................................................

.........................................................

*Create in me a new, **clean** heart, O God, filled with **clean** thoughts and **right desires**. (Psalm 51:10, TLB para-phrase)*

 WOW! According to the above scripture, God has the ability to give your heart and your mind a spiritual bubble bath. If you allowed Him to do that for you, what kind of difference would you notice?

..........................................................................

..........................................................................

..........................................................................

..........................................................................

*"Man looks at the **outward** appearance, but the LORD looks at the **heart**." (1 Samuel 16:7)*

 The above verse:

_____ a. Makes me feel relieved that God doesn't care if I'm having a bad hair day or if I forgot to use mouthwash.

_____ b. Challenges me to be sure to get my hair, clothes, and accessories just right.

_____ c. Challenges me to take a magnified look at

my heart to see if it's in solid spiritual shape.

_____ d. Helps me see that my heart is more important than being fashionable.

 What kinds of improvements do you think God wants to make inside your heart?

\_ \_ \_ \_ \_ \_ \_ \_ \_ \_ \_ \_ \_ \_ \_ \_ \_ \_ \_ \_ \_ \_ \_ \_ \_ \_ \_

\_ \_ \_ \_ \_ \_ \_ \_ \_ \_ \_ \_ \_ \_ \_ \_ \_ \_ \_ \_ \_ \_ \_ \_ \_ \_ \_

\_ \_ \_ \_ \_ \_ \_ \_ \_ \_ \_ \_ \_ \_ \_ \_ \_ \_ \_ \_ \_ \_ \_ \_ \_ \_

\_ \_ \_ \_ \_ \_ \_ \_ \_ \_ \_ \_ \_ \_ \_ \_ \_ \_ \_ \_ \_ \_ \_ \_

*What good things does God see when He peeks inside your daughter's heart?*

..........................................................................................

..........................................................................................

..........................................................................................

..........................................................................................

..........................................................................................

...........................................

*"Blessed are the **pure in heart**, for they will see God."* (Matthew 5:8)

Having a pure heart means:

_____ a. that I never have bad thoughts.

_____ b. that I go to church every week.

_____ c. that I do kind things for others.

_____ d. I've allowed God to truly be in charge and rule my heart. I've given ownership of my heart to Him.

Yeah, you can probably tell the right answer is the last one since it's the longest, right? It's true—when you give God ownership of your heart, His Holy Spirit will work inside you to create purity.

Soooo . . . who's holding your heart strings? Be honest! You? God? Someone else? What does that person have that makes you want to give him or her your heart?

........................................

........................................

........................................

............................................

..............................................

..............................................

..............................................

..............................................

..............................................

..............................................

If it's not God, why not? (Again! Be honest!)

..................................................................

..................................................................

..................................................................

..................................................................

Is there a noticeable difference in someone who's pure in heart and one who's not? Describe the difference.

..................................................................

..................................................................

..................................................................

..................................................................

..................................................................

..................................................................

The heart is actually the very center of a person's life. And guess what—this includes your mind, your will, and your emotions! Powerful, huh?

Why not go ahead and commit your entire **heart**—total control—to Christ right now? You can either pray this prayer for one another, separately, or together. And if this isn't something you can honestly do, ask God for the desire to give Him complete control of your heart.

Dear Jesus, thank You that You've already forgiven my sins and have given me new life. But Jesus, I struggle to give You complete control, especially when it comes to _____.
But I know I can't settle for giving You only 50 percent or even 98 percent of my life. I realize You want total control. You want

the reins of my life.

I've received Your forgiveness for my sins, but I still find myself calling my own shots. Oh, dear Jesus, will You forgive me? I want to give You 100 percent. I yield right now to Your authority. You have Your way in my life, okay? I give You my dreams, my relationships, my habits, my skills and abilities, my time, my money, my rights. I give You it all!

I'm even giving You the **unknown bundle**—all the stuff in my life that I don't even know about yet. The struggles I'll have next week. That tough time I'll encounter in a year. The friends I'll have five years from now. I'm giving You control of my past, my present, and my future.

Will You release the power of Your Holy Spirit within me? I want to live in **Your power**—not my own human strength. Cleanse me within. Sanctify me wholly. And help me live a godly life in Your power.

Thank You, Jesus, for helping me surrender everything to You. When I start to pick this stuff up again, gently remind me that it's no longer mine to hold. It's Yours. Thank You, Jesus! Amen.

closer

| Top 10 Most Popular Female Names in the 1900s | Top 10 Most Popular Female Names in the 1950s |
|---|---|
| Mary | Mary |
| Helen | Linda |
| Margaret | Patricia |
| Anna | Susan |
| Ruth | Deborah |
| Elizabeth | Barbara |
| Dorothy | Debra |
| Marie | Karen |
| Mildred | Nancy |
| Alice | Donna |

GAB FEST #3:

Just Chattin'

**O**kay, here's how this section works: Ask each other the
questions out loud. You can either answer aloud, or take
turns writing the answers down. Whatever you do, be
honest and have fun!

Mom, name three things you've noticed I'm good at.

_____

_____

_____

closer

*What things do you think I'm good at?*

.................................................................................
.................................................................................
.................................................................................

*What do you enjoy most about our home?*

.................................................................................
.................................................................................
.................................................................................

Mom, what makes you most proud of me?

_____

_____

_____

What things do I do that you hope you can do as well (or better) when you get older?

............................................

............................................

............................................

Mom, what's one of your favorite memories you have with me?

_____

_____

_____

Tell about one of your favorite memories you have of the two of us.

............................................

............................................

............................................

............................................

............................................

Mom, here's what I tell everybody about you when I'm bragging about you:

_____

_____

_____

*Is there something you wish you and I did together more often?*

...........................................................

...........................................................

...........................................................

Mom, what was the toughest thing for you about being a teenager?

_____

_____

_____

*Can you think of another mom/daughter relationship that you admire? Who are they, and what do you like about them?*

...........................................................

...........................................................

...........................................................

Take a moment and pray out loud for your mom. Ask God to bless your relationship and draw you closer together.

\_ \_ \_ \_ \_ \_ \_ \_ \_ \_ \_

\_ \_ \_ \_ \_ \_ \_ \_ \_ \_ \_

\_ \_ \_ \_ \_ \_ \_ \_ \_ \_ \_

\_ \_ \_ \_ \_ \_ \_ \_ \_ \_ \_

\_ \_ \_ \_ \_ \_ \_ \_ \_ \_ \_

\_ \_ \_ \_ \_ \_ \_ \_ \_ \_ \_

*Mom, take a moment and pray out loud for your daughter. Tell the Lord two things in her life that make you proud. Ask Him to bless this special time you're spending together.*

.....................................................................................

.....................................................................................

.....................................................................................

## Take a Break!

You deserve it. Look how much you've just completed. Whew! Have fun together. Go jump on a trampoline, play tennis, put a puzzle together, find a new word to both of you in the dictionary, whatever!

# Some Important Women in History

**Florence Nightingale** (1820 - 1910) Considered the founder of modern nursing, she worked on the battlefield during the Crimean War.

**Harriet Tubman** (1820 - 1913) Born a slave, she was an abolitionist and a conductor on the Underground Railroad. She led more than 300 slaves to freedom.

**Elizabeth Blackwell** (1821 - 1910) As the first woman physician, she founded the New York Infirmary for Women and Children in 1857 and the Women's Medical College in 1867.

**Emily Dickinson** (1830 - 1886) American poet.

**Louisa May Alcott** (1832 - 1888) She wrote many novels, including *Little Women* and *Little Men*, and worked to get voting rights for women.

**Carry Nation** (1846 - 1911) Famous for her work to ban alcohol.

**Charlotte E. Ray** (1850 - 1911) First African-American woman to get a law degree.

**Annie Oakley** (1860 - 1926) Rodeo star and sharpshooter. She was the star of Buffalo Bill's Wild West Show.

**Juliette Gordon Law** (1860 - 1927) Founded the American Girl Scouts.

**Anna Mary Robertson** "Grandma" Moses (1860 - 1961) This American painter sold her first painting when she was 78 years old.

**Elizabeth Cochrane Seaman** (1865 - 1922) Using her pen name, "Nellie Bly," she became famous for her articles exposing the conditions in mental hospitals and about her trip around the world in 72 days.

**Laura Ingalls Wilder** (1867 - 1957) This American writer authored the Little House on the Prairie books.

# Journal

 These are questions from Mom for you to answer right
here in this journal space.

✎ What's your favorite thing to eat that I cook?

_____

_____

✎ What do you wish I cooked more often?

_____

_____

✎ What's your favorite room in our home
and why?

_____

_____

✎ How can I make your life better?

_____

_____

✎ One more question (Mom, you choose):

_____

_____

# Journal

*Questions from your daughter for you to answer right here on this journal page.*

▭▶ If you could choose any period of time and history for our family to live in, what would you choose and why?

..........................................................................

..........................................................................

▭▶ What is the toughest thing about being a mom?

..........................................................................

..........................................................................

▭▶ If you could write a book about our family, what would you title it?

..........................................................................

..........................................................................

▭▶ How can I make your life easier?

..........................................................................

..........................................................................

▭▶ One more question (daughter, you choose):

..........................................................................

..........................................................................

# Back on Course

Grab your favorite gel pen and keep going! Take turns reading the following scriptures. Each time there's a change in paragraph, switch readers.

*Some time later, Jesus went up to Jerusalem for a feast of the Jews. Now there is in Jerusalem near the Sheep Gate a pool, which in Aramaic is called Bethesda and which is surrounded by five covered colonnades.*

*Here a great number of disabled people used to lie—the blind, the lame, the paralyzed. One who was there had been an invalid for thirty-eight years. When Jesus saw him lying there and learned that he had been in this condition for a long time, he asked him, "Do you want to get well?"*

*"Sir," the invalid replied, "I have no one to help me into the pool when the water is stirred. While I am trying to get in, someone else goes down ahead of me."*

*Then Jesus said to him, "Get up! Pick up your mat and walk."*

*At once the man was cured; he picked up his mat and walked. (John 5:1-9)*

The only reason these folks were at the pool was that they desperately wanted healing. There's a legend about this pool of Bethesda. The legend states that every now and then, an angel would stir the water. The first person to touch the water (or fall into it) while the water moved in this mysterious way would be healed.

There was probably a hot spring—or a sulfur spring—underground that caused the water to move. Imagine the crippled, diseased, and handicapped people crowding around the pool waiting for their chance to roll, crawl, or fall into the water. And imagine their disappointment when someone else beat them to the water.

Mom, describe a time when you hoped and hoped for something and it didn't happen. How did you feel? How did you work through it?

_____

_____

_____

_____

_____

_____

*Tell me about a time when you hoped for something and it didn't happen. How can I better help you through those times of disappointment?*

...........................................................................................

...........................................................................................

...........................................................................................

...........................................................................................

...........................................................................................

Jesus knows everything. He knew why the people were there, and He also knew how long each person had waited. So when he asked the paralyzed man if he wanted to get well, it must have seemed like a silly question at first.

Mom, what's one of the silliest questions I asked you when I was a child?

_____

_____

_What's the most important question you feel I've ever asked you?_

..................................................................

..................................................................

It may have seemed like a silly question Jesus asked the paralytic. But think about it. Thirty-eight years is a long time to lie around hoping for a miracle. Don't you think if he really wanted to get well, this man would have created a strategy? He could have asked his friends or family members to wait with him and drop him into the water when it moved.

What are some other strategies he could have come up with?

..................................................................

..................................................................

..................................................................

..................................................................

..................................................................

Hmmm. Could it be that the paralytic was afraid to get well? Perhaps he knew that if he was healed, everything would change. His physical body would change. His environment would change. How he lived his life would change. Change can be hard. Even good changes can sometimes be tough.

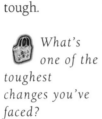 *What's one of the toughest changes you've faced?*

..................................................
..................................................
..................................................
..................................................

Mom, what's one of the toughest changes you've faced?

_ _ _ _ _ _ _ _ _ _ _ _ _ _ _ _ _ _ _ _ _ _

_ _ _ _ _ _ _ _ _ _ _ _ _ _ _ _ _ _ _ _ _ _

_ _ _ _ _ _ _ _ _ _ _ _ _ _ _ _ _ _ _ _ _ _

_ _ _ _ _ _ _ _ _ _ _ _ _ _ _ _ _ _ _ _ _ _

Mom, why are even good changes sometimes hard?

_ _ _ _ _ _ _ _ _ _ _ _ _ _ _ _ _ _ _ _ _ _

_____

_____

_____

*What changes would need to happen in our home for us to become completely whole?*

...................................................................

...................................................................

...................................................................

...................................................................

This man was paralyzed! What do you suppose he thought when Jesus commanded him to get up?

...................................................................

...................................................................

...................................................................

Describe a time in your life when it was difficult to obey Jesus. Did you end up obeying Him? If not, what kept you from obeying?

...................................................................

...................................................................

...................................................................

...................................................................

closer

Describe a time when you obeyed Jesus even though it seemed impossible at the time to do so.

..................................................................

..................................................................

..................................................................

..................................................................

The paralytic obeyed Jesus. And he was healed! He took his mat, got up, and went home.

In what ways can a person be paralyzed other than physically?

..................................................................

..................................................
..................................................
..................................................
..................................................
..................................................
..................................................
..................................................

Mom, do you see any areas in my life in which I'm emotionally paralyzed?

_____

_____

_____

Do you see any areas in my life in which I'm spiritually paralyzed?

_____

_____

_____

_____

_____

_____

_____

*closer*

*Are there areas in my life that seem emotionally or spiritually paralyzed?*

.........................................................................

.........................................................................

.........................................................................

Close your time together in prayer.

*Mom, pray for any areas in your daughter's life that you feel may be paralyzing her (or keeping her) from becoming all God wants her to be.*

 Pray for your mom. Ask God to strengthen her emotionally, physically, and spiritually.

## Take a Break!

Listen to your favorite radio station, listen to your heart beat, listen to your thoughts, listen to the wind, and keep going!

| Top 10 Most Popular Female Names in the 1970s | Top 10 Most Popular Female Names in the 1990s |
|---|---|
| Jennifer | Ashley |
| Amy | Jessica |
| Melissa | Emily |
| Michelle | Sarah |
| Kimberly | Samantha |
| Lisa | Brittany |
| Angela | Amanda |
| Heather | Elizabeth |
| Stephanie | Taylor |
| Jessica | Megan |

## Back on Course

Grab a rice cake and let's keep going!

*What's the toughest thing about being a teenager today?*

. . . . . . . . . . . . . . . . . . . . . . . . . . . . . . . . .

. . . . . . . . . . . . . . . . . . . . . . . . . . . . . . . . .

. . . . . . . . . . . . . . . . . . . . . . . . . . . . . . . . .

. . . . . . . . . . . . . . . . . . . . . . . . . . . . . . . . .

 Mom, what was something stupid you did as a teenager? Why did you do it?

What would you do differently if you could go back in time?

_____
_____
_____
_____

*What do you really enjoy about being a teenager today?*

...........................................................
...........................................................

Mom, what was difficult for you to talk with your mom about?

_____
_____

*What's difficult for you to talk with me about?*

...........................................................
...........................................................
...........................................................

Mom, if money and time weren't obstacles, what dream
would you want to fulfill?

_____
_____

closer

64

*If money weren't an obstacle, and you and I could go any-where in the world together, where would you want us to go? What would we do?*

·······························································································

·······························································································

·······························································································

Mom, when did you know beyond all doubt that you were a Christian?

— — — — — — — — — — — — — — — — — — — — — — —

— — — — — — — — — — — — — — — — — — — — — — —

— — — — — — — — — — — — — — — — — — — — — — —

*When did you decide you wanted to know Jesus? Who or what made the difference?*

.................................................................
.................................................................
.................................................................

Mom, what would you like me to pray about for you?

_ _ _ _ _ _ _ _ _ _ _ _ _ _ _ _ _ _ _ _ _ _ _ _ _
_ _ _ _ _ _ _ _ _ _ _ _ _ _ _ _ _ _ _ _ _ _ _ _ _
_ _ _ _ _ _ _ _ _ _ _ _ _ _ _ _ _ _ _ _ _ _ _ _ _
_ _ _ _ _ _ _ _ _ _ _ _ _ _ _ _ _ _ _ _ _ _ _ _ _

*What would you like me to pray about for you?*

.................................................................
.................................................................
.................................................................
.................................................................

## Take a Break!

You deserve it. Look how much you've just completed. Whew! Time for some fun. Go swimming, biking, napping, cooking, whatever!

# Quotes by Women

"Parents can only give good advice or put them [children] on the right paths, but the final forming of a person's character lies in their own hands."

**Anne Frank (1929–1945)**
*Anne Frank: The Diary of a Young Girl* **(1952), entry for July 15, 1944**

"We must not, in trying to think about how we can make a big difference, ignore the small daily differences we can make which, over time, add up to big differences that we often cannot foresee."

**Marian Wright Edelman**
*Families in Peril* **(1987)**

"You gain strength, courage and confidence by every experience in which you really stop to look fear in the face. You are able to say to yourself, 'I lived through this horror. I can take the next thing that comes along.' . . . You must do the thing you think you cannot do."

**Eleanor Roosevelt (1884–1962)**
*You Learn by Living* **(1960)**

# Quiz on Moms of the Bible

1. Who said to his mom, "Didn't you know I'd be about my Father's business?"

____ a. Samson          ____ b. Jesus

____ c. Paul            ____ d. Gideon

2. All of the following had a mom named Mary except one. Who was it?

____ a. James           ____ b. John Mark

____ c. Peter           ____ d. Jesus

3. Which mom talked her daughter into asking for John the Baptist's head on a platter?

____ a. Sapphira        ____ b. Jezebel

____ c. Lydia           ____ d. Herodias

4. Which king threatened to cut a child in half to discover who the baby's real mom was?

____ a. David           ____ b. Solomon

____ c. Saul            ____ d. Isaiah

5. Which mom was praying so intensely for God to give her a child that someone accused her of being drunk?

____ a. Hannah          ____ b. Sarah

____ c. Deborah         ____ d. Esther

6. Who said, "Naked I came from my mother's womb and naked I will depart"?

_____ a. Peter          _____ b. Andrew

_____ c. Job            _____ d. Uriah

7. Proverbs 23:22 gives some great advice on how to treat moms. It says, "Do not despise your mother when she is . . ."

_____ a. confused       _____ b. old

_____ c. wrong          _____ d. in labor

69

closer

1.b 2.c 3.d 4.b 5.a 6.c 7.b

# Back on Course

Share a laugh and keep going! Take turns reading the following passage. Each time there's a paragraph change, switch readers.

*Love is patient, love is kind.*

*It does not envy, it does not boast, it is not proud.*

*It is not rude, it is not self-seeking, it is not easily angered, it keeps no record of wrongs.*

*Love does not delight in evil but rejoices with the truth.*

*It always protects, always trusts, always hopes, always perseveres. (1 Corinthians 13:4-7)*

*Can you name some things I do that prove to you that I love you?*

.............................................................................

.............................................................................

.............................................................................

*Let me share with you some things I see in your life that demonstrate your love for our family:*

.............................................................................

.............................................................................

.............................................................................

.............................................................................

Mom, sometimes it's hard for me to be patient in loving others, like _____. How can I do better?

_____

_____

_____

Mom, tell me about a time when you were envious. How did you gain victory over the envy, and instead love and be glad for that person?

_____

_____

_____

_____

*Genuine love is protective. Can you think of some areas in which I demonstrate my love for you by being protective?*

. . . . . . . . . . . . . . . . . . . . . . . . . . . . . . . . . . . . . . . . . . . . . . . . . . . . . . . . . . . . . .

. . . . . . . . . . . . . . . . . . . . . . . . . . . . . . . . . . . . . . . . . . . . . . . . . . . . . . . . . . . . . .

. . . . . . . . . . . . . . . . . . . . . . . . . . . . . . . . . . . . . . . . . . . . . . . . . . . . . . . . . . . . . .

. . . . . . . . . . . . . . . . . . . . . . . . . . . . . . . . . . . . . . . . . . . . . . . . . . . . . . . . . . . . . .

Mom, sometimes I feel you're too protective, but genuine love trusts. How can I get over this feeling of you being too protective and simply trust your heart for me?

_____

closer

_____

_____

_____

 Mom, describe a time when you saw my love persevere.

_____

_____

_____

_____

*Will you pray for me to learn practical ways to show you*
*how much I love and care about you?*

 Mom, will you pray that my love will persevere through
tough times and especially when I find it difficult to trust?

## Take a Break!

You deserve it. Look
how much you've
just completed. Go
play the piano, play
the drums, play
Monopoly, or grab
some Play-Doh,
whatever . . . just
play!

## Achievements by Women

In November of 1999, **Randice-Lisa Altschul** was issued a series of patents for the world's first disposable cell phone. "Randi" patented her invention called the Phone-Card-Phone. It has the thickness of three credit cards and is made from recycled paper products.

Yes, it's a real cell phone! It contains 60 minutes of calling time, and it's disposable. When you've completed your 60 minutes, you can either purchase additional minutes or toss the phone in the trash.

**Bessie Blount** was a physical therapist who worked with injured soldiers in WW II. Her war service inspired her to patent a device in 1951 that allowed amputees to feed themselves.

The electrical device allowed a tube to deliver one mouthful of food at a time to a patient in a wheelchair or in a bed whenever he or she bit down on the tube. Bessie later invented a portable receptacle support that was a simpler and smaller version, designed to be worn around a patient's neck.

closer

# Quiz on Women of the Bible

1. What was the name of David's first wife?

____ a. Cindy      ____ b. Michal

____ c. Hagar      ____ d. Dinah

2. The book of Ruth is the first book of the Bible named after a woman. But who is Ruth's mother?

____ a. She isn't named.      ____ b. Naomi

____ c. Phoebe      ____ d. Dorcas

3. What's the name of John the Baptist's mom?

____ a. Sarai      ____ b. Esther

____ c. Vashti      ____ d. Elizabeth

4. Which woman was listed as a judge in the Bible?

____ a. Gomer      ____ b. Mary Magdalene

____ c. Deborah      ____ d. Rachel

5. Who sold purple cloth?

____ a. Jeptha      ____ b. Lydia

____ c. Deliah      ____ d. Naphtali

6. In the book of Acts, she and her husband lied to the church about the sale of their land.

____ a. Sapphira          ____ b. Eunice

____ c. Simone            ____ d. Jael

7. Why was Martha upset with Mary during Jesus' visit to their home?

____ a. Mary had her eye on Martha's guy.

____ b. Mary poured expensive perfume on Jesus' feet.

____ c. Mary was making fun of her brother, Lazarus.

____ d. Mary wasn't helping Martha prepare dinner.

# Back on Course

Give each other a hug and keep going!

*What three things would you like to accomplish in the next five years?*

........................................................................

........................................................................

........................................................................

........................................................................

Mom, when and how did you know what you wanted to do with your life?

_ _ _ _ _ _ _ _ _ _ _ _ _ _ _ _ _ _ _ _ _ _ _ _ _ _ _ _ _ _

_ _ _ _ _ _ _ _ _ _ _ _ _ _ _ _ _ _ _ _ _ _ _ _ _ _ _ _ _ _

_ _ _ _ _ _ _ _ _ _ _ _ _ _ _ _ _ _ _ _ _ _ _ _ _ _ _ _ _ _

_ _ _ _ _ _ _ _ _ _ _ _ _ _ _ _ _ _ _ _ _ _ _ _ _ _ _ _ _ _

_ _ _ _ _ _ _ _ _ _ _ _ _ _ _ _ _ _ _ _ _ _ _ _ _ _ _ _ _ _

*What can I do to make you feel more confident about your future?*

........................................................................

........................................................................

........................................................................

Mom, if you were offered a gift of knowing the future, would you accept it? Why or why not?

\_ \_ \_ \_ \_ \_ \_ \_ \_ \_ \_ \_ \_ \_ \_ \_ \_ \_ \_ \_ \_ \_ \_ \_

\_ \_ \_ \_ \_ \_ \_ \_ \_ \_ \_ \_ \_ \_ \_ \_ \_ \_ \_ \_ \_ \_ \_ \_

\_ \_ \_ \_ \_ \_ \_ \_ \_ \_ \_ \_ \_ \_ \_ \_ \_ \_ \_ \_ \_ \_ \_ \_

*What do you dislike about being a teenager? What are you looking forward to after graduation?*

.......................................................................................

.......................................................................................

.......................................................................................

*closer*

*What do I do that makes our relationship good? What can
I do to make our relationship better?*

..................................................................

..................................................................

..................................................................

Mom, what can I do to make our relationship better?

— — — — — — — — — — — — — — — — — — — — — —

— — — — — — — — — — — — — — — — — — — — — —

— — — — — — — — — — — — — — — — — — — — — —

Close this time together in prayer.

*Mom, pray for your daughter's future, her friends,
her goals, and your relationship with her.*

Pray for God to give your mom wisdom, guidance, and
confidence as she leads you as a mom. Pray He will grant
her wisdom and guide her future. Thank Him for allowing
the two of you to be together right here, right now, communicating as you are.

**Temptation: (Check all that apply.)**

❑ Hits me **harder** during the school year.

❑ Hits me harder during the **summer**.

❑ Is a **sin**.

❑ Happens to everyone—including **Jesus** when He lived on earth.

❑ Keeps me from becoming spiritually **victorious**.

❑ Doesn't become sin until **acted** upon.

❑ Hits me **hardest** at work.

❑ **Plagues** me at home.

❑ Hits me hardest at **night**.

GAB FEST #4:

# Tantalizing Temptations

closer

Take turns reading the following passage together.

*When tempted, no one should say, "God is tempting me." For God cannot be tempted by evil, nor does he tempt anyone; but each one is tempted when, by his own evil desire, he is dragged away and enticed.*

*Then, after desire has conceived, it gives birth to sin; and sin, when it is full-grown, gives birth to death. (James 1:13-15)*

Where does temptation come from?

.................................................................
.................................................................
.................................................................

Discuss an area of temptation each of you faced this week. How did you handle it?

.................................................................
.................................................................
.................................................................
.................................................................

What's the difference between temptation and sin?

_____ a. Sin happens when one gives in—or yields—to temptation.

_____ b. Temptation is an invitation to sin, but temptation itself is not sin.

*"And sin, when it is full-grown, gives birth to death"* (James 1:14). *When we give in to temptation, we sin. Does that mean we suddenly die? What kind of death is the apostle James talking about?*

## Take a Break!

You deserve it. Look how much you've completed. Go do a crossword puzzle, create a brand-new board game, sew a new pair of pants, whatever . . . just go do something!

No matter how much mothers and daughters love each other, sometimes they inadvertently do things that embarrass the other. And it seems as though often it's when one is trying to do something caring for the other!

**Read these stories to each other and have a good laugh!**

I was probably 14 years old. My mom and I were going to a movie together on a Saturday afternoon. There was a really cute guy working behind the counter, and of course since I was in junior high, any boy made me revert into a bundle of nerves. (This still often happens, but now I can pretend it doesn't.) I was trying to just stand there and smile, because that's about all I could handle. Then my mom ordered popcorn.

Cute Guy asked if we wanted butter. Mom asked me if I did

and I said, "No thanks." And I thought that was that. But then she turned around and looked at me—and it sounded like her voice was coming over a megaphone. (It was probably amplified by my 14-ness, but still!) She said, "Oh that's right. Buttered pop-corn gives you gas."

Cute Guy kind of chuckled. My face turned as red as my sweater. Mom claims it was more subtle than I remember. I don't think so.

—Natalie Lloyd, *Brio* Columnist

As a single girl in my 20s, I don't mind my mom's occa-sional schemes to set me up with a nice guy. One day, how-ever, she went a little too far. We were at a family reunion when she brought a very cute guy to the table where I was sitting with my brothers and their wives. She introduced Mr. Cute specifically to me—and no one else—in an obvious attempt to entice us in conversation. When it dawned on us that he was actually my cousin, I don't know which of us turned redder!

—Michelle McCorkle, *Brio* Designer

With seven kids to feed, my mom often took advantage of the quick, easy meals at fast-food restaurants. You can imagine the patience and talent it took to order for us all at a drive-thru. Once when we stopped at McDonald's, my  youngest sister asked for Coke with her Happy Meal. But when my mom turned to the speaker, she read from the menu board,

"One hamburger Happy Meal with a Coca-Cola Classic Enjoy."
From the backseats of our 12-passenger van, we all died laughing. But our mom didn't even realize what was so funny. She was too busy ordering the next "Cheeseburger Happy Meal with an Obey Your Thirst Sprite."

—Martha Krienke, *Brio* Assistant Editor

I was 13 and boarding the bus to go on a ski trip with our local ski club. Allow me to vividly paint this picture: 13-year-old me (who wants to fit in, wants to be cool, wants to sit in the good seats with the older kids) turns around after loading up my skis, and who's right behind me? Chad Ericson—the cutest boy on the trip and the best skier. This would seem like a perfect

opportunity to up my chances of sitting next to him on the bus in the cool seats, right? Wrong.

In the background, booming from the driver's seat of a '76 Jeep Wagoneer land-beast, is my mom, screaming, "LEXIE! DID YOU REMEMBER TO WEAR YOUR TRAINING BRA? SKIING MOGULS CAN BE REALLY HARD ON THAT . . . YOU KNOW . . . AREA!"

I thought I should probably just lie down in front of the bus and die of embarrassment. Instead, I sat up at the front of the bus with the chaperones and ski moms while everyone else played Uno in the back of the bus in the cool seats. Later . . . up on the mountain at the start of a very mogul-y ski run, Chad turns around and screams to the entire ski group, "I hope Lexie wore her training bra. This looks like a tough run!"

—Lexie Rhodes, *Brio* Senior Designer

In my freshman year of high school, I decided at the last minute to run for class secretary. My mother insisted that she help with the posters. She felt she had a clever idea about incorporating our name, Webb, in the posters, but didn't tell me what it was. I had my own ideas and wanted to do the posters myself. We had a fight about it, and I went to bed without making any. Mom stayed up all night and made 20 or so posters.

When I refused to take them to school, she "helpfully" took them for me and taped them up around school. I wanted to die when I saw what she'd done. Smack dab in the middle of every poster was a big, fat duck and the slogan said, "Everything's ducky when you vote for Webby." I didn't win the election.

—Susan Taylor Brown, author, *Oliver's Must-Do List*

How have I embarrassed you when I didn't mean to?

. . . . . . . . . . . . . . . . . . . . . . . . . . . . . . . . . . . . . . . . . . . . . . . . . . . . . . . . . . . . .

. . . . . . . . . . . . . . . . . . . . . . . . . . . . . . . . . . . . . . . . . . . . . . . . . . . . . . . . . . . . . . . . .

. . . . . . . . . . . . . . . . . . . . . . . . . . . . . . . . . . . . . . . . . . . . . . . . . . . . . . . . . . . . . . . . .

. . . . . . . . . . . . . . . . . . . . . . . . . . . . . . . . . . . . . . . . . . . . . . . . . . . . . .

# Back on Course

Give each other a big smile and keep going!

We often tend to think the way to handle temptation is to face it, stare it down. We think, *If I can look temptation right in the face and refuse to give in, I'll win the battle.* But that's not scriptural. We are not told anywhere in the Bible to handle temptation by facing it. Check out the strategy for temptation that the apostle Paul gave Timothy:

*But you, man of God, flee from all this, and pursue righteousness, godliness, faith, love, endurance and gentleness. (1 Timothy 6:11)*

And check out the strategy for dealing with temptation given to Lot and his family right before God destroyed Sodom and Gomorrah:

*"Flee for your lives! Don't look back, and don't stop anywhere in the plain! Flee to the mountains or you will be swept away!" (Genesis 19:17)*

Are you seeing the pattern? God doesn't want us to deal with temptation by facing it. He wants us to flee from it! *Merriam-Webster's Collegiate Dictionary*, Tenth Edition defines "flee" like this: **1 a** : to run away often from danger or evil : **FLY b** : to hurry toward a place of security.

I like that. "Hurry toward a place of security." We're to run the opposite direction, and not look back. Fly away from danger and evil. Get out of there as quickly as possible and get to a safe, secure place. That's how we're supposed to deal with temptation.

Here are some more verses to consider:

*Flee the evil desires of youth, and pursue righteousness, faith, love and peace, along with those who call on the Lord out of a pure heart. (2 Timothy 2:22)*

*Therefore, my dear friends, flee from idolatry. (1 Corinthians 10:14)*

*Flee from sexual immorality. All other sins a man commits are outside his body, but he who sins sexually sins against his own body. (1 Corinthians 6:18)*

Is this a different strategy for you? How do you usually handle temptation?

closer

Read 1 Timothy 6:11 again. As you're running away from temptation, what six things does the apostle Paul encourage you to pursue?

1. ..........................................................

2. ..........................................................

3. ..........................................................

4. ..........................................................

5. ..........................................................

6. ..........................................................

What does 2 Timothy 2:22 add to that list?

..............................................................

..............................................................

Mom, how do you see me pursuing righteousness in my life?

*Can you tell me how you see
endurance demonstrated in my life?*

...........................................................................
...........................................................................
...........................................................................

Mom, I think I'm pursuing faith by:

— — — — — — — — — — — — — — — — — — — —

— — — — — — — — — — — — — — — — — — — —

— — — — — — — — — — — — — — — — — — — —

— — — — — — — — — — — — — — — — — — — —

*The way I'm pursuing godliness is:*

...........................................................................
...........................................................................
...........................................................................

Share a time when you tried to handle temptation by
facing it instead of running from it. What happened?

...........................................................................
...........................................................................
...........................................................................
...........................................................................
...........................................................................

Mom, what was the greatest temptation you faced when you were my age? How did you deal with temptation then? How do you deal with it now?

_____

_____

_____

_____

_____

_____

*What's a common temptation that you face as a teen?*

..................................................

..................................................

..................................................

..................................................

## Take a Break!

Pray for each other right now. Ask God to help you flee temptation and pursue the qualities that He wants to develop in you.

# Unusual (but real) Female Names
## from A to (almost) Z

Which ones would you name your daughter? Which
would you never name your daughter?

..........................................................................

..........................................................................

- Abianne
- Affinity
- Amaryllis
- Ambrosia
- Baylyn
- Bettina
- Braelyn

- Cadence
- Camish
- Camisha
- Cashmere
- Coralee
- Crimson
- Damonica

- Davonte
- Ethereal
- Fauna
- Fennel
- Forsythia
- Glimmer
- Halcyon

- Harmony
- Hermetta
- Indigo
- Jae'won
- Jamari
- Jaquelle
- Katrita
- Kismet
- Laquan
- Liberty

- Meadow
- Mialyn
- Mimosa
- Nakeisha
- Osment
- Pleasant
- Promise
- Quantiko
- Quianna
- Reshawn

- Rhythm
- Serendipity
- Shawntika
- Silver
- Spruce
- Taffeta
- Tamarind
- Teal
- Trinity

## Back on Course

Let's dig a little deeper into the topic of temptation.

Grab your Bibles and flip to Matthew 26:41. What specifically did Jesus command His disciples to pray?

..................................................................

..................................................................

..................................................................

We probably don't pray against temptation often enough, do we? How would your life be different if you prayed daily to be kept from temptation?

..................................................................

..................................................................

The Lord's Prayer—the model Christ used to teach us how to pray—has a line about temptation in it. Turn to Matthew 6:13 and jot it down in your own words.

_____

_____

_____

_____

_____

_____

closer

Jesus was tempted, His disciples were tempted, and He knew we'd also be tempted. But He has given us a promise. Check this out:

*No temptation has seized you except what is common to man. And God is faithful; he will not let you be tempted beyond what you can bear. But when you are tempted, he will also provide a way out so that you can stand up under it. (1 Corinthians 10:13)*

What an incredible promise! When you're tempted, let this scripture remind you that you're not experiencing something no one else has ever experienced. You're not alone! And God will always provide a way of escape for you. How does this make you feel?

..................................................................................

..................................................................................

When you're being tempted, do you try to figure your own way out, or are you actively looking for God's escape plan?

..................................................................................

..................................................................................

## Take a Break!

Giggle till your sides hurt, eat a few chocolate chip cookies, or dance to your favorite tune on the radio. You deserve a break!

# Did You Know?

❀ Females have 500 more genes than males, and because of this, women are usually protected from color blindness and hemophilia.

❀ Men's shirts have the buttons on the right, but women's blouses have the buttons on the left. This is more than just a way to tell whether a shirt is for men or women. There's actually a historical reason for it.

During the Victorian period, buttons were quite expensive and were worn mostly by rich people. Since proper, well-to-do ladies were dressed by their servants, and most people are right-handed, their buttons were placed on the servant's right, which is the wearer's left side. However, most gentlemen dressed themselves, so their buttons were placed on the wearer's right side.

Those who couldn't afford servants copied the style of the wealthy, and women's buttons thereafter remained on the left.

❀ Years ago, parents began dressing their baby boys in blue because it was thought to prevent evil spirits from entering the boy's body. Blue was chosen because it's the color of the sky and was therefore associated with heavenly spirits.

Girls weren't dressed in blue because people didn't think that evil spirits would bother with them. Eventually, however, girls did get their own color. Pink was chosen because of an old English legend that said girls were born inside of pink roses.

❀ Women can talk longer with less effort than men. Know why? It's because our vocal cords are shorter than those of men, and we release less air through them to carry the sound. It's all a matter of breathing.

# Back on Course

**We've talked a lot about temptation. Let's put it into a real-life situation.**

Erica loved Josh's outgoing, life-of-the-party personality. She admired the way he included outsiders. He had a special gift of making everyone around him feel comfortable and special. He led their Christian fellowship group, and spoke openly about his faith. Everyone loved Josh. Erica was grateful for the special friendship they'd shared through their high school years and now beyond. She respected his faith and how he lived it.

As the College Christian Fellowship party began to wind down, Josh grabbed his jacket and turned to Erica. "Need a ride home?" he said. "I'm going your way."

"Sure. Thanks, Josh."

They climbed into his bright red Jeep and headed out of the church parking lot. "Mind if I make a quick stop?" Josh asked.

"Of course not."

A few minutes later, they pulled into a grocery-store parking lot. "I'll leave the motor running," he said. "I'll just be a sec."

"No problem," Erica said. "I've got your iPod to keep me company."

She scrolled through the play lists and finally landed on something she liked as Josh opened the door and placed a six-pack of beer in the backseat.

"Okay. To your house."

"Josh, what are you doing with beer?"

"Gonna have a few drinks after I drop you off," he said.

"But Josh . . . you don't drink."

"You don't think I drink," he said. "I've been drinking for a couple of years now. It's no big deal."

"Yes, it is a big deal! Just because we're out of high school now, doesn't mean you should turn your back on everything you've been taught and have believed."

"Look, Erica. We've both been in church our whole lives.

We've both heard the warnings about drinking. But it's not like I'm hurting anyone else when I'm drunk. I don't drink and drive. I don't drink in front of anyone. It's just something I do when I'm alone."

"So no one even knows you drink?"

"Right."

"And you don't think that's hypocritical?" she said.

"Yeah, it probably is a bit hypocritical," he admitted. "But I'm still gonna do it."

"Wait a sec. I remember you speaking out in youth group one night . . . saying that God had told you drinking was wrong."

"Yeah. That was what—three years ago? Good memory, Erica! I know what I'm doing doesn't make God happy, but I still wanna do it. And I'm still gonna do it."

"But, Josh, it's wrong. I know it's wrong for me, and you know it's wrong for you. We've both talked about how God definitely let us know that drinking wasn't in His will for us."

"I know, Erica. And I'm not gonna argue with you."

Erica couldn't believe it. *He knows what he's doing is wrong*, she thought, *yet he keeps doing it. I don't really know what to say!*

As they turned the corner to her house, Erica noticed her parents weren't home yet.

"Looks pretty dark," Josh said. "You gonna be okay?"

"Yeah, they're not back yet."

"And I'll bet you stopped carrying a house key when you left for college, right?" Josh teased.

"Right."

"And now that you're home on spring break, you forgot to start carrying the key again!"

"Right again," Erica said. "But I can get in through the pad on the garage door. I do remember our keyless entry code."

"Want me to keep you company for a while?"

"Aren't you in a hurry to get home and start putting away your six-pack?"

"Yeah . . . but since no one's here, I could start slow with just one . . . and even share if you're interested."

Erica swallowed. Josh was a family friend. Even though her parents had strict rules about not letting guys in the house while they were gone, they trusted Josh. *Well, they trust the Josh they think they know*, she thought.

"Yeah, I don't know, Josh. You know my parents and the house rules, and they're gone and—"

"It's me—Josh! Your old buddy. Your folks love me. I've been over here lots of times."

"Yeah, but my parents have always been home when you've been here."

"I won't stay long. Besides, don't you think I should make sure everything's safe?"

*I know Mom and Dad wouldn't want Josh inside while they're away,* Erica reasoned. *And they'd never allow alcohol.*

"Come on," Josh pleaded. "We're college freshmen—adults now!"

"All right," she said. "But only for a little bit. My parents will probably be home in a few hours."

Josh turned off the engine, grabbed the six-pack, and followed Erica through the garage. An hour and a half later, they'd devoured the six-pack.

 Josh and Erica both knew it was wrong for them to drink, yet they did it anyway. According to the following definition of sin, did they sin?

**For a person claiming to be a Christian, sin is deliberately going against the known will of God.**

_____ Yes _____ No

At what point did temptation begin for Erica?

...............................................................................

...............................................................................

Erica seemed so adamant against drinking. What do you think Josh said to convince her to try it?

...............................................................................

...............................................................................

What else could Erica have said to Josh when she saw him bring the six-pack out of the store and place it in the backseat of the Jeep?

_____

_____

*How would you have reacted to coming home and finding Josh there against your house rules?*

. . . . . . . . . . . . . . . . . . . . . . . . . . . . . . . . . . . . . . . . . . . . . . . . . . . . . . . . . . . . .

. . . . . . . . . . . . . . . . . . . . . . . . . . . . . . . . . . . . . . . . . . . . . . . . . . . . . . . . . . . . .

Was it Josh's fault or Erica's fault that he came inside?

_____

*What could Erica have said when Josh invited himself inside? What could she have said when he insisted?*

. . . . . . . . . . . . . . . . . . . . . . . . . . . . . . . . . . . . . . . . . . . . . . . . . . . . . . . . . . . . .

. . . . . . . . . . . . . . . . . . . . . . . . . . . . . . . . . . . . . . . . . . . . . . . . . . . . . . . . . . . . .

What could Erica have done to refuse giving in to temptation?

. . . . . . . . . . . . . . . . . . . . . . . . . . . . . . . . . . . . . . . . . . . . . . . . . . . . . . . . . . . . .

. . . . . . . . . . . . . . . . . . . . . . . . . . . . . . . . . . . . . . . . . . . . . . . . . . . . . . . . . . . . .

. . . . . . . . . . . . . . . . . . . . . . . . . . . . . . . . . . . . . . . . . . . . . . . . . . . . . . . . . . . . .

What should Erica do now?

.............................................................

.............................................................

.............................................................

Have you been in a similar situation?
How did you handle it?

.............................................................

.............................................................

.............................................................

.............................................................

.............................................................

closer

 Go back and reread 1 Corinthians 10:13 and 1 Timothy 6:11. How could things have been different for Erica if she'd leaned on the truth found in these scriptures?

...........................................................................

...........................................................................

...........................................................................

*Close this time together by praying for your daughter. Ask God to give her wisdom when she's tempted. Ask Him to help her lean on His strength to run away from the temptation.*

 Thank God for His promise to always help you escape temptation. Ask Him to teach you to depend on Him when you're tempted. If you need to seek His forgiveness for giving in to temptation, you can do that now.

## Important Dates in Women's History

**1847** – Maria Mitchell, first American woman astronomer, discovers a new comet.

**1861** – Julia Ward Howe writes the words to "The Battle Hymn of the Republic."

**1864** – Sojourner Truth visits President Lincoln at the White House.

**1881** – Clara Barton establishes the American Red Cross.

**1891 – 1893** – Lydia Liliuokalani reigns as Queen of Hawaii.

**1904** – Helen Keller graduates from Radcliffe.

**1912** – Girl Guides (Girl Scouts) is founded in America.

**1983** – Sally Ride becomes the first American woman to fly in space.

**1917** – Jeannette Rankin becomes the first woman to be elected to the U.S. Congress.

**1920** – United States women win the right to vote.

**1946** – Eleanor Roosevelt is elected chairperson of the United Nations Human Rights Commission.

**1972** – Shirley Chisholm is the first African-American woman to serve in Congress.

**1973** – Barbara Jordan becomes the first African-American woman from a Southern state to serve in Congress.

**1988** – Jackie Joyner-Kersee wins two Olympic gold medals.

**1990** – Oprah Winfrey becomes the first woman to own and produce her own syndicated television show.

# GAB FEST #5:
# Real Love

Ready for a good love story? Jacob was definitely in love! Rachel sent his heart racing like no one else. He admired her love for God, her commitment to her family, and her warm personality. He asked her father, Laban, if he could marry her. Laban agreed he could marry Rachel after Jacob worked seven years for him. Jacob could hardly contain his excitement. He loved her so much, those years were worth it.

Are you familiar with the term "delayed gratification"? It means wanting something really really really badly, but being willing to wait until the time is right. For example, a guy and girl may be in love and yearn to express their feelings through physical intimacy. But they decide to wait until after they're married, because they want God's best. They're delaying their gratification.

Let's say you've just finished two hours of volleyball practice, and you're driving home. Your mom told you this morning as you left for school that she'd have pot roast and a freshly baked chocolate cake for dinner. You've been looking forward to it all day.

But you're so hungry right now, you decide to stop at McDonald's on your way home. *I don't want to wait another 20 minutes for dinner,* you think. So you gratify your desires immediately, and doing so ruins your dinner. Later you wish you'd waited.

*You and your husband have had the same kitchen table since you were married 15 years ago. He told you this morning that in three months he'll get a bonus, and you'll be able to purchase that brand-new dining room table you've been wanting. You're so excited, you decide "just to look" this after-noon. You see the exact table you want. Why wait three months? you think. We can make monthly payments. I know the money will be here within three months.*

*You purchase the table on credit. Your husband loves the table, but he wishes you'd waited for his bonus, so you wouldn't have to pay interest until he receives it. His disappointment causes tension between you. You're sad that you hurt the relationship when three months was not really a long time to wait.*

*Identify a time in your life when you delayed your gratifi-cation for the best result.*

..................................................................

..................................................................

..................................................................

..................................................................

..................................................................

Identify a time in your life when you wished you'd delayed your gratification for greater results.

— — — — — — — — — — — — — — — — — — — — — — —

— — — — — — — — — — — — — — — — — — — — — — —

— — — — — — — — — — — — — — — — — — — — — — —

**W**hat an incredible love story! The man of her dreams, sweating and working hard for her hand in marriage. You can imagine how excited Jacob and Rachel were when the seven years finally ended. They'd made it! But before you accept an invitation to the wedding, you'd better check out the entire story in Genesis 29:16-30. Go ahead and read it. I'll wait . . .

closer

Done?

You sure?

Okay.

I'll bet you can imagine the scene: Jacob dressed in a fancy black tuxedo with a silver cummerbund. His hair cut neatly around his ears. Just the right dab of cologne.

The organ plays. In walks the bride. Her face is covered with her beautifully laced veil, and she glides toward the altar with a bouquet of fresh flowers in her hands. The ceremony continues, they are pronounced husband and wife. He leads her to his tent. It's dark outside, and even darker inside the tent. They spend their first night together.

When Jacob wakes up the next morning and turns to look at his wife, he yells. It's not Rachel! It's her older sister, Leah!

Laban wanted his older daughter to marry first, so he tricked Jacob. "You can still marry Rachel," he said. "But you'll need to work another seven years for me."

At this point, would you be tempted to forget "delayed gratification" and give in to your desires? (Or be so furious you'd punch Laban?)

Describe a time in your life when you were deceived or tricked out of something you were looking forward to. How did you work through it?

---------------------------------

---------------------------------

---------------------------------

*Why is it best to delay your gratification in most situations?*

.................................................

.................................................

.................................................

How have fast food, microwaves, high-speed Internet, call waiting, and overnight shipping influenced our thinking about delayed gratification?

.................................................

.................................................

List three areas in your life in which you know God wants you to delay gratification.

---------------------------------

---------------------------------

---------------------------------

---------------------------------

*List three areas in your life in which you know God wants you to delay gratification.*

.................................................

........................................................................................

........................................................................................

........................................................................................

Jacob agreed to work for Laban another seven years for the hand of Rachel in marriage. What does this say about the love he had for Rachel?

........................................................................................

........................................................................................

........................................................................................

Can you identify someone in your life who has loved you like this?

........................................................................................

........................................................................................

## Take a Break!

Go kayaking, go window-shopping, go around the block, but take a break! And have fun with the next couple of pages.

Mom, your daughter has a lot on her mind! Try to place yourself in her shoes, and prioritize the jobs in the order of their importance.

1. _____

2. _____

3. _____

4. _____

1. Update iPod play list.
2. Enter today's journal notes in blog.
3. Call Jessica.
4. Paint toenails.

Circle the correct answers.

Which of the following items is not essential to housecleaning?

Which of the following should be a priority?

Which of the following should be done on a regular basis?

 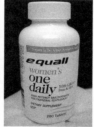  

**Study this picture for 30 seconds. Strive to remember every detail of the mom and daughter.**

**Now, answer the following questions:**

*1. Who's the lead singer of U2?*

.................................................................

*2. What's the difference between an iPod and an MP3 player?*

.................................................................

 1. If you're feeling stressed, which vitamin can help alleviate tension?

— — — — — — — — — — — — — — — — — — — — — — — —

2. At what temperature and for how long should you cook a tuna casserole?

— — — — — — — — — — — — — — — — — — — — — — — —

# Back on Course

Let's talk a little more about real love.

 How can you see real love demonstrated in the following couples found in the Bible?

· Abraham and Sarah (Genesis 17–23; see especially Genesis 23:2)

· Ruth and Boaz (Ruth 2–4)

· Hosea and Gomer (Hosea)

How do you want the man of your dreams to demonstrate genuine love to you?

_____

_____

_____

_____

_____

*How has genuine love been demonstrated to you?*

. . . . . . . . . . . . . . . . . . . . . . . . . . . . . . . . . . . . . . . . . . . . . . .

. . . . . . . . . . . . . . . . . . . . . . . . . . . . . . . . . . . . . . . . . . . . . . .

. . . . . . . . . . . . . . . . . . . . . . . . . . . . . . . . . . . . . . . . . . . . . . .

. . . . . . . . . . . . . . . . . . . . . . . . . . . . . . . . . . . . . . . . . . . . . . .

How will you demonstrate genuine love to your future husband?

_____

_____

_____

_____

*How are you currently demonstrating genuine love in your relationship with your husband? (If you aren't married, think of a close friend or child.)*

...................................................................

...................................................................

...................................................................

Oftentimes people confuse lust with love. It's easy to believe that sexual desire equals love. It doesn't. Love is willing to sacrifice. Lust is "my needs." Love will wait (delay gratification). Lust is impatient.

What are some other differences between lust and love?

...................................................................

...................................................................

...................................................................

...................................................................

List three TV shows or movies that highlight lust.

. . . . . . . . . . . . . . . . . . . . . . . . . . . . . . . . . . . . . . . . . . . . . . . . . . . . . . .

. . . . . . . . . . . . . . . . . . . . . . . . . . . . . . . . . . . . . . . . . . . . . . . . . . . . . . .

. . . . . . . . . . . . . . . . . . . . . . . . . . . . . . . . . . . . . . . . . . . . . . . . . . . . . . .

List three TV shows or movies that highlight real love.

. . . . . . . . . . . . . . . . . . . . . . . . . . . . . . . . . . . . . . . . . . . . . . . . . . . . . . .

. . . . . . . . . . . . . . . . . . . . . . . . . . . . . . . . . . . . . . . . . . . . . . . . . . . . . . .

. . . . . . . . . . . . . . . . . . . . . . . . . . . . . . . . . . . . . . . . . . . . . . . . . . . . . . .

 Mom, how can I tell if a guy is in love with me or is simply in lust with me?

_____

_____

_____

*Pray for your daughter's future husband and family.*

Pray that God will be making you the lady your future husband and children will need. Pray for your mom to show real love to her husband.

# Take a Break!

Make up a new word, make your bed, make cookies, make time to take a break, and make yourself enjoy the next few pages!

closer

 **Stuff You Probably Won't Hear Your Mom Say Anytime Soon**

"Honey, you seem tired this morning. Were you up late doing your homework again? I'll have a talk with your teacher and try to get her to ease up, okay? If that doesn't work, I'll go to the principal. And if you're still getting homework, I'll make an appointment with the school superintendent!"

"The important thing isn't that I've spent two hours on dinner. I just can't believe I forgot you don't like brussels sprouts. Forget dinner with the family. Here's some money for a pizza. You get whatever you want."

"I've been thinking. If Dad and I don't take a vacation this year, we'll have just enough money to buy a plasma flat-screen television for your bedroom!"

"Sweetie, you deserve a shopping spree! Take my credit card and have fun."

"You're feeling cramped? We'll rent you a furnished apartment. We trust you. And don't worry about the bills. We'll take care of them."

"Yes, the presidential debate started 10 minutes ago. Your father and I are certainly enjoying it. Oh, wait a second! I forgot that your favorite cable show is on right now. Come on in and sit down. We can read about the debate in tomorrow morning's paper. We don't want you to miss out on your show!"

"No, you don't have to save your money. We want you to spend your baby-sitting cash on a new iPod."

## Stuff You Probably Won't Hear Your  Daughter Say Anytime Soon

"Mother, is there anything you want to ask me? I'd be happy to tell you anything you want to know."

"Brittany and I were going to play putt-putt tonight, but I'd rather stay home and clean the house for you. Would that be okay?"

"Mom, I really appreciate the allowance you give me. But I can actually do with less gas money. It won't hurt me to walk to school a few times each week."

"I've been saving for three months to go to summer camp, but I don't mind putting it off until next year so I can go on vacation with you and Dad. You could probably use my help in sorting through Aunt Helena's ceramic collection. It's so thoughtful of her to invite our entire family to stay in her one-bedroom apartment during July."

"Is my music too loud? I don't mind turning it down a few decibels if it's bothering you."

"Mom, you look a little weary. Let me fix you a warm bubble bath while I whip something up for dinner."

"I can't wait till Friday night! I'm really looking forward to staying in and devoting the whole evening to meaningful conversation."

"Mom, do you think my room is clean enough? I really want to set a good example for my brothers and sisters."

# Back on Course

As we continue our discussion about real love, think seriously about the following discussion questions.

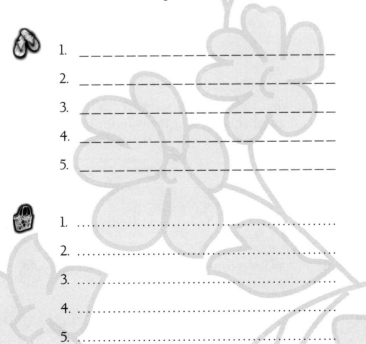

Mom, what qualities do you see in me that will benefit my future marriage?

_____

_____

_____

_____

*Let's each take a few minutes to think of the five most important things a woman should look for in a husband. Then we'll compare notes, okay?*

1. _____

2. _____

3. _____

4. _____

5. _____

1. .................................................

2. .................................................

3. .................................................

4. .................................................

5. .................................................

*Now let's both take a few minutes to list the top five things*
*you shouldn't tolerate in a future spouse.*

closer

1. _____

2. _____

3. _____

4. _____

5. _____


1. ...................................................................

2. ...................................................................

3. ...................................................................

4. ...................................................................

5. ...................................................................


Mom, what are a couple of spiritual qualities you see in
me that I can bring to my future home?

_____

_____

_____


*What are a couple of spiritual qualities that you see me*
*demonstrate in our home?*

...................................................................

..............................................

..............................................

*What are some spiritual qualities you want in your future husband?*

..............................................

..............................................

..............................................

What are some spiritual qualities you admire in Dad (or a man you respect)?

‑ ‑ ‑ ‑ ‑ ‑ ‑ ‑ ‑ ‑ ‑ ‑ ‑ ‑ ‑ ‑ ‑ ‑ ‑ ‑ ‑ ‑

‑ ‑ ‑ ‑ ‑ ‑ ‑ ‑ ‑ ‑ ‑ ‑ ‑ ‑ ‑ ‑ ‑ ‑ ‑ ‑ ‑ ‑

‑ ‑ ‑ ‑ ‑ ‑ ‑ ‑ ‑ ‑ ‑ ‑ ‑ ‑ ‑ ‑ ‑ ‑ ‑ ‑ ‑ ‑

What's the best thing about your marriage?

‑ ‑ ‑ ‑ ‑ ‑ ‑ ‑ ‑ ‑ ‑ ‑ ‑ ‑ ‑ ‑ ‑ ‑ ‑ ‑ ‑ ‑

‑ ‑ ‑ ‑ ‑ ‑ ‑ ‑ ‑ ‑ ‑ ‑ ‑ ‑ ‑ ‑ ‑ ‑ ‑ ‑ ‑ ‑

‑ ‑ ‑ ‑ ‑ ‑ ‑ ‑ ‑ ‑ ‑ ‑ ‑ ‑ ‑ ‑ ‑ ‑ ‑ ‑ ‑ ‑

*What do you see in our marriage that you'd like to also see in your own marriage?*

..............................................

..............................................

..............................................

## Close in prayer together.

 Ask God to spiritually strengthen your future husband and to begin making him the spiritual leader you'll need in your future home.

*Thank God for your daughter and all that she has to offer her future family. Ask God to spiritually strengthen her now to become all her family will need someday.*

## Take a Break!

Brush your hair, have a brush with adventure, brush against your cat, or take a break and enjoy the next page.

## The Top 10 Countries
## Where Women Outnumber Men

1. Cape Verde

2. Latvia

3. Ukraine

4. Antigua

5. Belarus

6. Bulgaria

7. Lithuania

8. Russia

9. Cambodia

10. Moldova

closer

# Journal

What have you learned from this gab fest on real love?

_____

_____

_____

_____

_____

_____

_____

_____

_____

_____

_____

_____

_____

_____

_____

_____

_____

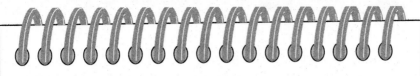

# Journal

*What do you hope your daughter remembers most from this gab fest on real love? What can you do to help make this happen?*

..........................................................................................

..........................................................................................

..........................................................................................

..........................................................................................

..........................................................................................

..........................................................................................

..........................................................................................

..........................................................................................

..........................................................................................

..........................................................................................

..........................................................................................

..........................................................................................

..........................................................................................

..........................................................................................

..........................................................................................

..........................................................................................

..........................................................................................

..........................................................................................

### Did You Know?

· Women in New Zealand were the first in the world to obtain the right to vote in 1893.

· Cinderella's slippers were originally made out of fur. The story was changed in the 1600s by a translator. It was the left shoe that Cinderella lost at the stairway, when the prince tried to follow her.

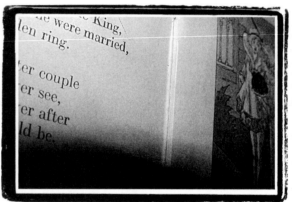

· Emmeline Pankhurst founded the Women's Franchise League in Britain in 1889, which fought to allow married women to vote in local elections. She died in 1928, just weeks after the Voting Rights for Men and Women Act was passed.

· Barbie's full name is Barbara Millicent Roberts.

· Barbie's measurements if she were life-size: 39-23-33.

· Men do 29 percent of the laundry each week. Only 7 percent of women trust their husbands to do it correctly.

· What do bullet-proof vests, fire escapes, windshield wipers, and laser printers all have in common? They were all invented by women.

## GAB FEST #6:

# Making Wise Choices

Every day, all day long, we're making choices. Sometimes they're big choices, sometimes they're small. Sometimes we don't even realize the choices we're making will have far-reaching effects into our future, or the futures of others. Sometimes making the right choice can be tough—in part because we might not know what the right choice is, or because we know what the right choice is, but just don't want to do it.

Before we look at some biblical

principles about decisionmaking and wisdom, why don't you guys have fun discussing the following choices.

closer

## Would you rather:

❑ eat a package of uncooked microwave popcorn

OR

❑ eat a box of uncooked spaghetti?

##  Would you rather:

❑ hiccup for three straight days

OR

❑ wear all your clothing backward for three straight days?

## Would you rather:

❑ cut a city block of grass with your teeth

OR

❑ lick up a 12-foot-by-12-foot rain puddle?

**Would you rather:**

❑ do five jumping jacks every time someone says hi to you for the rest of your life

OR

❑ gargle with lemon juice 30 minutes a day every day for the rest of your life?

 **Would you rather:**

❑ have to have medical attention because you have a marble stuck in your nose

OR

❑ need help because your head is stuck between the bars of an iron fence?

 **Would you rather:**

❑ have brown teeth

OR

❑ have a hairline just one inch above your eyebrows?

**Would you rather:**

❑ always wear shoes that are a half-size too small

OR

❑ drink a gallon of water every day left from cooking hot dogs?

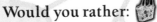

**King Solomon was one of the wisest men to have ever lived. Check this out: (Read out loud, alternating each paragraph.)**

*God gave Solomon wisdom and very great insight, and a breadth of understanding as measureless as the sand on the seashore.*

*Solomon's wisdom was greater than the wisdom of all the men of the East, and greater than all the wisdom of Egypt.*

*He was wiser than any other man, including Ethan the Ezrahite—wiser than Heman, Calcol and Darda, the sons of Mahol. And his fame spread to all the surrounding nations.*

*He spoke three thousand proverbs and his songs numbered a thousand and five.*

*He described plant life, from the cedar of Lebanon to the hyssop that grows out of walls. He also taught about animals and birds, reptiles and fish.*

*Men of all nations came to listen to Solomon's wisdom, sent by all the kings of the world, who had heard of his wisdom. (1 Kings 4:29-34)*

Solomon was wise in the areas of botany, sea life, language, music, and many other things. Verse 29 says that he also had a "breadth of understanding." What does that mean?

. . . . . . . . . . . . . . . . . . . . . . . . . . . . . . . . . . . . . . . . . . . . . . . . . . . . . . . .

. . . . . . . . . . . . . . . . . . . . . . . . . . . . . . . . . . . . . . . . . . . . . . . . . . . . . . . .

. . . . . . . . . . . . . . . . . . . . . . . . . . . . . . . . . . . . . . . . . . . . . . . . . . . . . . . .

Describe a situation in which you really wanted to understand something, but just didn't quite "get it."

..............................................................................

..............................................................................

..............................................................................

Is there a difference between being smart and having common sense? Describe each.

..............................................................................

..............................................................................

..............................................................................

..............................................................................

..............................................................................

closer

Is it possible to have one of those qualities without having the other?

..............................................................................

*Which do you think you have more of: common sense or knowledge? Which do you think your daughter has?*

..............................................................................

..............................................................................

Which do you think you have more of? Which do you think your mom has?

_____

_____

_____

## Take a Break!

Memorize a Bible verse, memorize the laugh lines on your face, or memorize the fun facts on the next few pages.

# Famous Firsts by American Women

**1707** Henrietta Johnston begins to work as a portrait artist in Charles Town (now Charleston), South Carolina, making her the first known professional woman artist in America.

**1767** Anne Catherine Hoof Green takes over her late husband's printing and newspaper business, becoming the first American woman to run a print shop. The following year she's named the official printer for the colony of Maryland.

**1809** Mary Kies becomes the first woman to receive a patent, for a method of weaving straw with silk.

**1853** Antoinette Blackwell becomes the first American woman to be ordained a minister in a recognized denomination (Congregational).

**1864** Rebecca Lee Crumpler becomes the first African-American woman to receive an M.D. degree. She graduated from the New England Female Medical College.

**1946** Edith Houghton becomes the first woman hired as a major-league baseball scout.

**1866**    Lucy Hobbs becomes the first woman to graduate from dental school—the Ohio College of Dental Surgery.

**1873**    Ellen Swallow Richards, the first woman to be admitted to the Massachusetts Institute of Technology, earns her B.S. degree. She becomes the first female professional chemist in the United States.

**1885**    Sarah E. Goode becomes the first African-American woman to receive a patent, for a bed that folded up into a cabinet. She owned a furniture store in Chicago and intended the bed to be used in apartments.

**1887**    Susan Medora Salter becomes the first woman elected mayor of an American town, in Argonia, Kansas.

**1901**    On October 24, 1901, Annie Edison Taylor, a schoolteacher from Michigan, becomes the first person to go over Niagara Falls in a barrel.

**1925**    Nellie Tayloe Ross becomes the first woman to serve as governor of a state, Wyoming.

**1926**    American Gertrude Ederle becomes the first woman to swim across the English Channel.

**1932**    Amelia Earhart becomes the first woman to fly solo across the Atlantic, traveling from Harbor Grace, Newfoundland, to Ireland in approximately 15 hours.

**1932**    Hattie Wyatt Caraway, of Arkansas, becomes the first woman elected to the U.S. Senate.

**1967**    Althea Gibson is the first African-American tennis player to win a singles title at Wimbledon.

**1972**    Juanita Kreps becomes the first woman director of the

New York Stock Exchange. She later becomes the first
woman appointed Secretary of Commerce.

**1981**   Sandra Day O'Connor is appointed by President
Reagan to the Supreme Court, making her its first
woman justice.

**1990**   Dr. Antonia Novello is sworn in as U.S. Surgeon
General, becoming the first woman (and first
Hispanic) to hold that job.

**1993**   Toni Morrison becomes the first African-American
woman to win the Nobel Prize for literature.

**1999**   Lt. Col.
Eileen
Collins is the
first woman
astronaut to
command a
space shuttle
mission.

**2005**   Condoleezza
Rice
becomes the
first African-
American
female
Secretary of
State.

# Back on Course

closer

Let's keep moving in the direction of making right choices!

Read the story of King David and Bathsheba in 2 Samuel 11, even if you know it well.

Have you done it?

Well, go on. I'll wait.

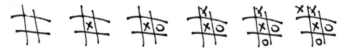

Okay. What did you see?

Not very pretty, is it?

Can you imagine? This is just one book away from 1 Samuel 13:14 (NASB) where Samuel tells Saul (referring to David),

*The LORD has sought out for Himself a man after His own heart, and the LORD has appointed him as ruler over His people.*

David, a man after God's own heart, commits adultery with Bathsheba, then has her husband killed. Whew! How did that happen?

Let's look back. David's bad choices didn't begin with that act of adultery. He didn't wake up one morning thinking, *I'll sin today by having an affair with a married woman.*

Do you wake up in the morning ready to sin? Probably not. In fact, rarely does anyone wake up and simply decide to sin.

Temptation comes before sin, and it comes in sugarcoated packages. In other words, temptation will always look, feel, or sound enticing. Think about it: If it wasn't enticing, you wouldn't be tempted.

Sometimes temptation comes in small, tiny, baby steps. We take one tiny step at a time, choosing to compromise in small areas of our lives. It's not long, however, before those small areas lead to much bigger areas.

Let's trace a few of King David's steps through the poor choices he made.

**Step 1:** David got up from his bed and went to the roof of his palace. This may have been as innocent as you getting up in the night and going into the kitchen to look inside the fridge. Perhaps he was restless and just wanted some air.

Once he reached the roof, however, he saw a beautiful woman bathing.

What was David's first temptation? What was his first, small compromise? What are some things David could have/should have done instead of giving in to that temptation?

_____

_____

_____

_____

*Describe a time when you could have/should have chosen something different but instead yielded to temptation. What was the first, almost innocent step? What was the first, seemingly small compromise? What have you learned from that experience?*

..................................................
..................................................
..................................................

How can what your mom learned help you make right
choices with your own life?

_ _ _ _ _ _ _ _ _ _ _ _ _ _ _ _ _ _ _ _ _ _ _ _

_ _ _ _ _ _ _ _ _ _ _ _ _ _ _ _ _ _ _ _ _ _ _ _

_ _ _ _ _ _ _ _ _ _ _ _ _ _ _ _ _ _ _ _ _ _ _ _

**Step 2:** David watched the woman bathe and admired
her beauty. He then sent someone to find out who she
was. Here was David's critical point number two. He
could have gone back to his room and sought the Lord's forgiveness for watching a woman bathe; instead he obviously continued to think about what he'd seen until he made the choice to
learn her identity.

*Now that David is determined to discover the beautiful
woman's identity, how will that play into further temptation to do something more?*

..................................................
..................................................

Why would it have been a better choice for David never
to learn the woman's identity?

_ _ _ _ _ _ _ _ _ _ _ _ _ _ _ _ _ _ _ _ _ _ _ _

_____

_____

Share a time in your lives when you found out something you later wished you didn't know.

........................................................

........................................................

........................................................

........................................................

**Step 3:** David was told her name was Bathsheba. Her husband, Uriah, was fighting in the war. Upon learning her husband was away, David then sent for her.

Ooooh! Bad decision number three. If you were David's friend, what would you say to him about his decision to invite Bathsheba over? How would you try to talk him out of it? Or would you? What would have been a better choice for him at this point?

........................................................

........................................................

........................................................

**Step 4:** David then slept with Bathsheba. Yowza. Doesn't that make you want to jump up and down and yell at David? "Don't be so stupid! What were you thinking?"

How many times have you realized you made a hugely bad mistake—when it was too late? How do you think David felt?

..........................................................................

..........................................................................

..........................................................................

Let's think back to the first step David took: He was probably surprised to see a woman bathing when he stood on his roof. At that point, if we could have pulled him aside and said, "Better go back to bed, David, or you'll end up having an affair with this woman," David probably would have laughed at how absurd that was. He wasn't thinking about having an affair when he went outside onto the roof.

 Discuss how one step of compromise can lead to other steps of compromise in the following areas:

a first drink of alcohol at a party—alcoholism;

cheating in school—cheating on taxes;

allowing other activities to become more important than going to church—attending church only once or twice a year;

skirting the truth—lying to a friend, spouse, employer, or parent.

**Step 5**: Bathsheba tells David she is pregnant with his child.

*At this point, what could/should David have done?*

.....................................................................................

.....................................................................................

.....................................................................................

When have you felt you were in a situation that was way over your head? Was it a result of poor choices you'd made? When have you felt so confused that making a good decision seemed impossible to figure out?

— — — — — — — — — — — — — — — — — — — —

— — — — — — — — — — — — — — — — — — — —

— — — — — — — — — — — — — — — — — — — —

**Step 6**: David's pretty trapped, isn't he? When we get into similar situations, we, like David, often continue to make poor choices, hoping to hide our sin.
David calls Bathsheba's husband, Uriah, home from war for a couple of days. He presumed Uriah was like most men—eager to sleep with his wife. Then everyone, including Uriah, would assume the baby born later was his.

Some people might think this was a smart move; a way to hide the truth. Describe how this deception contradicts David as being a man of integrity.

— — — — — — — — — — — — — — — — — — — —

_ _ _ _ _ _ _ _ _ _ _ _ _ _ _ _ _ _ _ _ _ _ _ _ _ _ _ _

_ _ _ _ _ _ _ _ _ _ _ _ _ _ _ _ _ _ _ _ _ _ _ _ _ _ _ _

**144**

closer

**Step 7:** Uriah refused to stray from how he felt a warrior should behave. As long as his comrades suffered on the battlefield, he wouldn't allow himself the comforts they lacked and longed for—home and a sweet wife. When David realized Uriah wouldn't cooperate with his deceitful plan, he made another bad choice: He got Uriah drunk, assuming now he'd go home and sleep with his wife. But Uriah slept on the floor among the servants.

Can you describe a time in your life when someone around you compromised or made poor choices, but you continued to act with integrity? Or when you wished you'd been the one acting with integrity?

_ _ _ _ _ _ _ _ _ _ _ _ _ _ _ _ _

_ _ _ _ _ _ _ _ _ _ _ _ _ _ _ _ _

_ _ _ _ _ _ _ _ _ _ _ _ _ _ _ _ _

_ _ _ _ _ _ _ _ _ _ _ _ _ _ _ _ _

_ _ _ _ _ _ _ _ _ _ _ _ _ _ _ _ _

**Step 8:** David, probably frantic at being caught, acted out of desperation and commanded that Uriah be placed at the front lines on the battlefield so he'd be more likely to die in the war. How did David go from taking an evening stroll to planning a murder?

Describe a situation where someone you know went from one small, ordinary event to a step of compromise through a series of bad choices, as David did.

.................................................................

.................................................................

.................................................................

.................................................................

.................................................................

**Step 9:** When Bathsheba learned her husband had been killed, the Bible tells us that she mourned. After her mourning, David brought her to his palace and married her. She bore him a son who later became ill and died. Take a peek at 2 Samuel 11:27: "But the thing David had done displeased the LORD." That sounds almost like an understatement, doesn't it?

After Uriah died, things didn't get better, did they? David's choices still had long-term consequences. What are some of them? (Read further about David if you wish to see how far-reaching his choices went into his future.) What choices have you made (good or bad) that you have seen reach much further into the future than you expected? What does this tell you about the importance of all your choices—from small to large?

.................................................................

.................................................................

.................................................................

.................................................................

Nathan, a prophet of the Lord, confronted King David with his sin. When David was approached by Nathan, he:

___ a.   denied his sin.
___ b.   rationalized his sin.
___ c.   fired Nathan.
___ d.   admitted his sin.

Though David made some severely bad choices, he finally had a chance to make a good decision, and he did! In 2 Samuel 12:13, we read, "Then David said to Nathan, 'I have sinned against the LORD.'" He took responsibility for his actions and admitted what he'd done. He didn't try to rationalize, or reason it through, or explain what he did. He simply admitted his responsibility for his own choices—sinful choices.

Describe a time when you made a series of bad decisions but finally turned around and made a good choice. What made the difference? Was there someone who helped you make a good decision? If so, what did that person do that was helpful?

...............................................................................

...............................................................................

...............................................................................

...............................................................................

*Tell your daughter about a time when you took responsibility for your own actions—as embarrassing and difficult as it was. Tell her what you learned and why it's important to take that responsibility.*

...............................................................................

...............................................................................

......................................

......................................

......................................

......................................

......................................

......................................

One of the most exciting things about serving God is that He has the power and the desire to make good things happen out of bad situations. He can take our history of poor choices and give us a brand-new start by empowering us to make good decisions!

Share a time you quickly made a decision on your own and later realized you should have waited on the Lord and sought His direction.

‒ ‒ ‒ ‒ ‒ ‒ ‒ ‒ ‒ ‒ ‒ ‒ ‒ ‒ ‒ ‒ ‒ ‒ ‒ ‒ ‒ ‒ ‒

‒ ‒ ‒ ‒ ‒ ‒ ‒ ‒ ‒ ‒ ‒ ‒ ‒ ‒ ‒ ‒ ‒ ‒ ‒ ‒ ‒ ‒ ‒

‒ ‒ ‒ ‒ ‒ ‒ ‒ ‒ ‒ ‒ ‒ ‒ ‒ ‒ ‒ ‒ ‒ ‒ ‒ ‒ ‒ ‒ ‒

‒ ‒ ‒ ‒ ‒ ‒ ‒ ‒ ‒ ‒ ‒ ‒ ‒ ‒ ‒ ‒ ‒ ‒ ‒ ‒ ‒ ‒ ‒

*Share a time when you sought God's direction, and He*
*helped you make the right decision.*

......................................

closer

Did God forgive David? How did you come to that conclusion? Even though David's decisions carried long-reaching consequences, what else did God bring into his life?

## Take a Break!

Curl your hair, put your hair up, let your hair down, cut your hair, or forget your hair and enjoy the following trivia.

# Did You Know?

**How long did it take her to wash and dry her hair?** She had really long hair! Her name was Xu Huiqin. She was a Chinese woman whose hair was 69 inches long!

**Watch out for the scratches!** The longest fingernails in the world belonged to Lee Redmond of Salt Lake City, Utah. They were 261 inches!

**Woman holds record for longest fall survived in an elevator.** Betty Lou Oliver, an elevator operator, survived a plunge of 75 stories (that's more than 1,000 feet!) in an elevator in the Empire State Building on July 28, 1945.

**Only the animals know for sure.** An old law that was never removed from the books in Raleigh, North Carolina, states that before a man asks for a woman's hand in marriage, he must be "inspected by all the barnyard animals on the young woman's family's property, to ensure a harmonious farm life."

**Perfect timing.** Ralph and Carolyn Cummins had five children between 1952 and 1966. All were born on February 20th.

**No spa needed.** Catherine the Great relaxed by being tickled.

# Back on Course

Let's keep hiking toward making wise choices.

closer

The Bible has a lot to say about wisdom. Take turns reading and discussing the following scriptures.

*The fear of the LORD is the beginning of wisdom. (Psalm 111:10)*

*What does it mean to fear the Lord? Are we supposed to be scared of Him?*

.....................................................................

.....................................................................

.....................................................................

*If any of you lacks wisdom, he should ask God, who gives generously to all without finding fault, and it will be given to him. (James 1:5)*

*How does God give wisdom? What does it look like? Sound like?*

.....................................................................

.....................................................................

.....................................................................

What area in your life would you love to have some wisdom in right now?

– – – – – – – – – – – – – – – – – – – – – – – – – – –

_____

_____

*Stop and pray for this specific area in your daughter's life,*
*and ask God to give her His wisdom and discernment.*

But the wis-
dom that comes
from heaven is first
of all pure; then
peace-loving, con-
siderate, submis-
sive, full of mercy
and good fruit,
impartial and sin-
cere. (James 3:17)

*How does*
*this list help*
*you see whether or*
*not the wisdom we*
*receive is really*
*from God?*

. . . . . . . . . . . . . . . . . . . . . . . . . . . . . . . . . . . . . . . . . . . . . . . . . . . . . . .

. . . . . . . . . . . . . . . . . . . . . . . . . . . . . . . . . . . . . . . . . . . . . . . . . . .

How can wisdom be peace-loving? Considerate? Give an
example from something that has happened with your
friends at church or school.

_____

_____

*closer*

*What does it mean that the wisdom God gives will be full of mercy or good fruit? Give an example from your life.*

.............................................................
.............................................................
.............................................................
.............................................................

Think of an example to share with your mom about how the wisdom she shares with you reflects that which "comes from heaven."

— — — — — — — — — — — — — — — — — — — — — —
— — — — — — — — — — — — — — — — — — — — — —
— — — — — — — — — — — — — — — — — — — — — —
— — — — — — — — — — — — — — — — — — — — — —

*Share with your daughter a time when you saw how she took God's wisdom and applied it to her life.*

.............................................................
.............................................................
.............................................................

## Take a Break!

You deserve it. Make popcorn balls, Rice-Krispie treats, or brownies and share them with another family member.

# Famous Females in Television and Literature QUIZ

1. Who was Beaver Cleaver's mom?

. . . . . . . . . . . . . . . . . . . . . . . . . . . . . . . . . . . . . . . . . . . . . . . . . . . . . . . . . . . . .

2. Who did Mr. Darcy truly love in *Pride and Prejudice*?

. . . . . . . . . . . . . . . . . . . . . . . . . . . . . . . . . . . . . . . . . . . . . . . . . . . . . . . . . . . . .

3. Which character in *Little Women* loved to write?

. . . . . . . . . . . . . . . . . . . . . . . . . . . . . . . . . . . . . . . . . . . . . . . . . . . . . . . . . . . . .

4. Who are the five friends in the Brio Girls book series?

. . . . . . . . . . . . . . . . . . . . . . . . . . . . . . . . . . . . . . . . . . . . . . . . . . . . . . . . . . . . .

5. Who was the female anchor on *20/20* for several years?

. . . . . . . . . . . . . . . . . . . . . . . . . . . . . . . . . . . . . . . . . . . . . . . . . . . . . . . . . . . . .

6. What's the name of the elf princess who is in love with Aragorn in J.R.R. Tolkien's *The Lord of the Rings*?

. . . . . . . . . . . . . . . . . . . . . . . . . . . . . . . . . . . . . . . . . . . . . . . . . . . . . . . . . . . . .

7. Who is the author of the Christy Miller series?

. . . . . . . . . . . . . . . . . . . . . . . . . . . . . . . . . . . . . . . . . . . . . . . . . . . . . . . . . . . . .

8. Who is the other famous Christy in literature?

.........................................

9. Who was the lead character in *Jane Eyre*?

.........................................

10. What was Velvet's last name in *National Velvet*?

.........................................

# Back on Course

Onward, march! We're traveling in the direction of making wise choices.

We've chatted about making good and bad choices, but what about those times when we know what the right decision is, and yet we purposefully make a wrong choice? Identify a time in each of your lives when this has happened.

..................................................................

..................................................................

..................................................................

..................................................................

Check this out: "*Anyone, then, who knows the good he ought to do and doesn't do it, sins*" *(James 4:17)*.

OUCH!

How can you more purposefully allow God to help you make wise choices?

..................................................................

..................................................................

..................................................................

..................................................................

..................................................................

..................................................................

Share a time when you knew beyond any doubt that God gave you the wisdom you needed to make the right decision.

.......................................................................
.......................................................................
.......................................................................
.......................................................................
.......................................................................

*How can God's wisdom help you make good choices?*

.......................................................................
.......................................................................
.......................................................................

*Do not be wise in your own eyes; fear the LORD and shun evil.*
*(Proverbs 3:7)*

Share a time when you acted on your own wisdom and it backfired.

— — — — — — — — — — — — — — — — — — —
— — — — — — — — — — — — — — — — — — —
— — — — — — — — — — — — — — — — — — —
— — — — — — — — — — — — — — — — — — —
— — — — — — — — — — — — — — — — — — —
— — — — — — — — — — — — — — — — — — —

 *According to the above scripture, how can learning to fear the Lord help us to shun evil?*

..........................................................................................

..........................................................................................

 What does "shun" mean? And how can shunning evil help us make wise choices?

_____

_____

*Rebuke a wise man and he will love you. (Proverbs 9:8)*

closer

Why would a wise person welcome rebuke?

_____

_____

_____

Identify a time in each of your lives when you wisely
accepted rebuke, and it benefited you.

...........................................................

...........................................................

...........................................................

...........................................................

...........................................................

...........................................................

*He who walks with the wise grows wise. (Proverbs 13:20)*

How does being around wise people make you wiser? How does
being around the foolish make you more likely to choose poorly?

_____

_____

_____

_____

*Point out a time in your daughter's life when she was the wise person who influenced those hanging out with her.*

..............................................................................

..............................................................................

Why does who we hang with truly affect us? Is it possible to hang with people and not allow them to affect us at all?

_____

_____

_____

_____

_____

*For the foolishness of God is wiser than man's*
*wisdom. (1 Corinthians 1:25)*

closer

Who is the wisest person you know? What makes him/her wise? What would it mean to say that this person's wisdom is still lacking when stacked against God's foolishness?

_____

_____

_____

_____

## Take a Break!

You deserve it. Grab a Coke, take off your shoes, wiggle your toes, go find a swing and see who can fly the highest, whatever!

## What Are You Cooking? QUIZ

Ok, you're both in the kitchen stirring and mixing a variety of ingredients. Identify what you're making.

1. You're mixing flour and salt. You add some cold shortening with a pastry cutter. Next you add cold water and mix quickly. What are you making?

    \_\_\_a. pie crust
    \_\_\_b. biscuits
    \_\_\_c. cookies
    \_\_\_d. muffins

2. You're layering wide flat noodles with cheese and tomato sauce. Next, you top it with more cheese, and you bake it. What are you making?

    \_\_\_a. lasagna
    \_\_\_b. risotto
    \_\_\_c. polenta
    \_\_\_d. spaghetti carbonara

3. You're mixing flour, baking powder, and salt. You cut in some cold shortening, then you add milk. You mix and knead 10 times. What are you making?

___a. play dough

___b. cookies

___c. biscuits

___d. muffins

4. You've made something that's served "cordon bleu." What will your dish be?

___a. set on fire

___b. stuffed with cheese and ham

___c. raw

___d. covered with marinara sauce

5. You poached eggs on slices of ham. Then you put both on English muffins. Now you're pouring hollandaise sauce on top. What are you serving?

___a. scrambled eggs

___b. huevos rancheros

___c. an omelet

___d. eggs Benedict

6. You're beating butter, eggs, and sugar together. You gradually add mixed dry ingredients. What are you making?

___a. pancakes

___b. French toast

___c. cookies

___d. a cake

7. Some of your ingredients are coriander, lemongrass, and fish sauce. What are you cooking?

___a. Mexican cuisine

___b. Southeast Asian cuisine

___c. East African cuisine

___d. Italian cuisine

8. You're mixing one cup of flour with one-half cup of salt. Next, you add three tablespoons cream of tartar and then one cup of water and two tablespoons of oil. You cook it over medium heat. What are you making?

___a. cream soup

___b. béarnaise sauce

___c. muffins

___d. play dough

Answers:

1.a 2.a 3.c 4.b 5.d 6.c 7.b 8.d

# Back on Course

How can having a strong, intimate, growing relationship with God help you make wise choices?

_____

_____

_____

God is the source of wisdom. So it only makes sense that the more time you spend with Him, and the more you study His Word, the wiser you'll become. What will you need to change in your schedule to make more room for consistent Bible study and time with the Lord?

. . . . . . . . . . . . . . . . . . . . . . . . . . . . . . . . . . . . . . . . . . . . . . .

. . . . . . . . . . . . . . . . . . . . . . . . . . . . . . . . . . . . . . . . . . . . . . .

. . . . . . . . . . . . . . . . . . . . . . . . . . . . . . . . . . . . . . . . . . . . . . .

. . . . . . . . . . . . . . . . . . . . . . . . . . . . . . . . . . . . . . . . . . . . . . .

Study the following scenario and discuss how Megan can make the right decision by seeking God's wisdom.

Megan's best friend is attending Central Baptist University and wants Megan to join her after high school graduation. "We'll have so much fun together," Krista says. "We'll room together and join the choir and do all kinds of fun stuff. And you'll love our dorm Bible study. It's awesome!"

Having Christian professors who know her by name, instead of being merely a number, sounds great to Megan. She

also likes the idea of being on a Christian campus surrounded by other Christians. *People often meet their future spouse in college,* she thinks. *So what better place to meet a good Christian guy than at a Christian university?*

While Megan is leaning toward attending Central Baptist, she's also considering a state school. *On a secular campus I could really shine bright for Christ,* she thinks. *I'd certainly have some challenges and debates with professors and students who aren't Christians, but they could strengthen me and teach me how to defend my faith. Perhaps there are students I could invite to non-threatening Christian events and open the door to share my faith with them.*

Should Megan solidify her relationship with Christ by attending a Christian university? She'll grow spiritually through chapel services and in being taught by Christian professors.

Or should she attend a state campus and allow God to use her as "salt" to bring a Christlike flavor to those who don't know Him? She could still grow spiritually by getting involved in a Christian group on campus. She may even win some of her classmates to the Lord.

The more she thinks about it, she can see how God can use her and help her grow spiritually in both situations. How can she make the right decision?

closer

What are some other advantages of Megan attending a Christian university?

_____

_____

_____

_____

_____

*What are some other advantages of Megan attending a state university?*

....................................................

....................................................

....................................................

....................................................

....................................................

What are the disadvantages of both?

....................................................

....................................................

....................................................

....................................................

....................................................

....................................................

Eventually, how will Megan be able to discern God's will and make the wisest choice possible?

.................................................................................

.................................................................................

.................................................................................

How might God help you make the best possible choices in the following areas:

dating

— — — — — — — — — — — — — — — — — — — — —

— — — — — — — — — — — — — — — — — — — — —

deciding what to study in college

— — — — — — — — — — — — — — — — — — — — —

— — — — — — — — — — — — — — — — — — — — —

friendships

— — — — — — — — — — — — — — — — — — — — —

— — — — — — — — — — — — — — — — — — — — —

how to spend your money

— — — — — — — — — — — — — — — — — — — — —

— — — — — — — — — — — — — — — — — — — — —

how to spend your time

— — — — — — — — — — — — — — — — — — — — —

— — — — — — — — — — — — — — — — — — — — —

*closer*

*How might God help you make the best possible choices in the following areas:*

family decisions

..............................................................

..............................................................

work

..............................................................

..............................................................

vacation

..............................................................

..............................................................

how to spend your money

..............................................................

..............................................................

how to spend your time

..............................................................

..............................................................

## Take a Break!

You deserve it. Make a root-beer float, see if you can still jump rope, talk about your favorite movie, whatever!

## Miscellaneous Quiz About a Variety of Women

1. Who played Blair on the TV show, *Facts of Life*?

2. Which actress played the roles of Lena in a movie and Rory on a TV show?

3. Who wrote "America the Beautiful"?

4. What was the name of the woman caught in adultery in the Bible? Jesus sent her accusers away.

5. Which book and chapter in the Bible describes an "ideal" woman? (a) Psalm 139  (b) Ruth 5  (c) Proverbs 31

6. What was the name of Cain's mother?

7. What's the name of Ray Barone's wife on the TV show *Everybody Loves Raymond*?

8. What celebrity went from starring in her own TV show, to recording a CD, to film acting?

9. What well-known Christian female singing group is comprised of four women who went to college together and currently do events for teen girls besides concert tours?

10. What's the name of the woman who is head of the National Day of Prayer?

1. Lisa Whelchel 2. Alexis Bledel 3. Katherine Bates 4. No one knows for sure. 5. (c) Proverbs 31 6. Eve 7. Debra Barone or Patricia Heaton 8. Hilary Duff 9. Point of Grace 10. Shirley Dobson

closer

# Back on Course

Let's jot some thoughts on paper.

## Journal

 What stands out most in this last section about making wise choices? What areas of your life do you struggle with the most in making wise choices?

-------------------------------------

-------------------------------------

-------------------------------------

-------------------------------------

-------------------------------------

-------------------------------------

-------------------------------------

-------------------------------------

-------------------------------------

-------------------------------------

-------------------------------------

-------------------------------------

-------------------------------------

-------------------------------------

## Journal

*What stands out most in this last section regarding making wise choices? How do your choices affect your daughter? How can you guide her in making wise decisions?*

...........................................................................

...........................................................................

...........................................................................

...........................................................................

...........................................................................

...........................................................................

...........................................................................

...........................................................................

...........................................................................

...........................................................................

...........................................................................

...........................................................................

...........................................................................

...........................................................................

...........................................................................

...........................................................................

...........................................................................

...........................................................................

closer

*Do you pray for and with your daughter? What has God taught you through prayer about your daughter?*

.....................................................................................

.....................................................................................

.....................................................................................

.....................................................................................

What has God taught you through your mom about
making decisions?

_____

_____

_____

_____

_____

_____

_____

_____

_____

_____

_____

_____

_____

_____

_____

_____

_____

_____

closer

Congrats! You did it! You finished the entire book together. Now how about considering meeting together consistently for special mom/daughter dates to discuss the Bible, your lives, and share prayer requests? There's a lot of power in prayer! Don't simply pray for each other. Make every effort to also pray with one another.

*Write a short note to your daughter highlighting what you've learned about yourself and her through this journey.*

.........................................................................................
.........................................................................................
.........................................................................................
.........................................................................................
.........................................................................................
.........................................................................................
.........................................................................................

Write a short note to your mom highlighting what you've learned about yourself and her through this journey.

_ _ _ _ _ _ _ _ _ _ _ _ _ _ _ _ _ _ _ _ _ _ _ _ _ _ _ _ _ _ _ _
_ _ _ _ _ _ _ _ _ _ _ _ _ _ _ _ _ _ _ _ _ _ _ _ _ _ _ _ _ _ _ _
_ _ _ _ _ _ _ _ _ _ _ _ _ _ _ _ _ _ _ _ _ _ _ _ _ _ _ _ _ _ _ _
_ _ _ _ _ _ _ _ _ _ _ _ _ _ _ _ _ _ _ _ _ _ _ _ _ _ _ _ _ _ _ _
_ _ _ _ _ _ _ _ _ _ _ _ _ _ _ _ _ _ _ _ _ _ _ _ _ _ _ _ _ _ _ _
_ _ _ _ _ _ _ _ _ _ _ _ _ _ _ _ _ _ _ _ _ _ _ _ _ _ _ _ _ _ _ _